The Art of

Timeless Étiquette,

Graceful Dining Manners,

&

Afternoon Tea

Copyright © 2020   Bernadette Michelle Petrotta

All rights reserved.

No part of this book may be reproduced by any mechanical, photographic, or electronic process or otherwise be copied for public or private use without the written permission of the author, Bernadette Michelle Petrotta.

ISBN: 978-0-9888742-2-0

The Art of

Timeless Étiquette,

Graceful Dining Manners,

&

Afternoon Tea

Featuring

Social Graces ~ Étiquette History
Introduction Methods ~ Entertaining Guidelines
Correspondence Protocol ~ History of Tableware
Dining Out Manners ~ American and Continental Dining
Appropriate Dress Attire ~ History of Tea ~ Types of Tea
Tea Pairings and Tastings ~ Tea Food Dining Instructions
Formalities for Preparing a "Proper" Afternoon Tea

Étiquette Series Volume IV

Bernadette Michelle Petrotta
Polite Society School of Étiquette

Also Authored by
Bernadette Michelle Petrotta

The Art of the Social Graces
Volume I

The Art and Proper Étiquette
of Afternoon Tea
Volume II

EMMA The Étiquette Cat:
Meet Emma
Volume III

Ce livre à pour objectif de regrouper l'ensemble des bonnes manières, également appelées étiquette.

This book aims to bring together all the good manners, also called étquette.

Dedication

I express my gratitude to my mother, Sarah L. Petrotta—a gracious and loving mom.
I think loving thoughts of her daily.

To my husband, Jens O. Rivera, who is extremely supportive of all my endeavors.
You are a gifted writer and you continue to fill my heart with your love.

To my son, Christopher A. Nicastro, and his wife, Pascale L. Mager—
you both are so loving, very accomplished, and exceptionally talented.

Jens O. Rivera – Editor
Michael Stadler – Photographer
Kelsey R. Hoff – Illustrator and Layout Designer
A special thank you to Karen Eaton.

Table of Contents

Foreword	xiii
About the Author	xv
About the Book	xvi
Brief History of Étiquette	1
Introduction Methods	3
The Art of Conversation	5
Easy Entertaining	7
Formal Dining	15
Informal Dining	25
Family Dining	28
Buffet Dining	30
Additional Entertaining Guidelines	37
Gracious Dining with Flowers, Beautiful Table Settings, and Fine Linens	43
Alfresco Entertaining	45

Table of Contents

Flatware	47
Flatware Design	49
Dinnerware	55
Dinnerware History	57
Crystal	61
Stemware	63
Dining Out	65
Graceful Dining Manners	69
Additional Dining Guidelines	89
Your Professional Life	91
Virtues	95
Appropriate Dress Attire	99
Personal Grooming	101
Thank-You Notes	103

Table of Contents

History of Tea	105
Influences in the World of Tea	109
Afternoon Tea in England	111
Styles of Tea	115
Camellia Sinensis	119
Types of Tea	121
Tea Pairings	125
Tea Tastings	129
Preparing a "Proper" Tea at Home	131
Making a Perfect Pot of Tea	135
Dining with Savories	143
Dining with Scones	145
Dining with Petits Fours	147
Enjoying Tea from a Teapot in a Teahouse or Restaurant	151
Enjoying Tea from a Teacup in a Teahouse or Restaurant	153

Foreword

By Jens O. Rivera

My first impression of Bernadette was her beauty. Once I got beyond the lovely exterior, her elegance and grace stirred my bachelor curiosity, so I commenced upon an extended courtship, paying particular attention to my p's and q's. It was a successful engagement and after twenty years of marriage, I am still learning from her the social graces and especially an appreciation of the finer aspects of culture.

Bernadette's latest book, *The Art of Timeless Étiquette, Graceful Dining Manners, & Afternoon Tea,* is an exceptional source of information covering highly developed common-sense rules and manners for everyday living and elaborate social occasions. Whether with time-tested materials, such as the chapter on virtues, or how to handle difficult party foods, this book takes the reader through all areas of étiquette history, dining, tea, entertaining, and much more. I am not quite as polished as the Prince of Wales, but my lovely wife is a wonderful teacher who continues to patiently coax me into developing the finer points of social skills and manners, and I remain her earnest and life-long student.

Bernadette Michelle Petrotta
Polite Society School of Étiquette

About the Author

Ms. Bernadette Michelle Petrotta is an author and a small business owner. She is married and has a son. After receiving her degree, she spent thirty-two years in public service with the City of Los Angeles in an administrative capacity. In her spare time, she researched the world of étiquette and eventually amassed a library of materials including a collection of rare silver flatware and antique porcelain serving pieces. In 1996, she founded the *Polite Society School of Étiquette* with a mission to educate people of all ages in customary codes of conduct, dining principles, and basic social skills. *Polite Society School of Étiquette* offers online courses, webinars, and tutelage at speaking engagements, school seminars, private dinners, and specialty tea events.

As a testament to Ms. Petrotta's dedication to étiquette, she was featured in *Tea Time Magazine* and *Texas Tea & Travel Magazine*. Ms. Petrotta provided first-class étiquette training along with educational classes on tea and its rich history to the personnel at the Fairmont Olympic Hotel in Seattle. She has also been a highlighted speaker at the Annual Northwest Tea Festival, Annual Victoria Tea Festival, Annual Northwest Women's Show, and Designs for Dining Fundraiser. She is listed in the business register of the International Tea Sipper's Society which reaches tea lovers worldwide.

Ms. Petrotta's entrepreneurial spirit, continuing education, and high-quality teaching principles qualify her to be a leading source in this rapidly expanding industry.

Ms. Petrotta has published four volumes in her Étiquette Series.

Volume I	*The Art of the Social Graces*
Volume II	*The Art and Proper Étiquette of Afternoon Tea*
Volume III	*EMMA The Étiquette Cat: Meet Emma*
Volume IV	*The Art of Timeless Étiquette, Graceful Dining Manners, & Afternoon Tea*

Available in Hardcover, Softcover, and eBook formats at www.PoliteSocietySchool.com.

About the Book

The *Polite Society School of Étiquette* presents Volume IV, *The Art of Timeless Étiquette, Graceful Dining Manners, & Afternoon Tea,* featuring Social Graces, Étiquette History, Introduction Methods, Entertaining Guidelines, Correspondence Protocol, History of Tableware, Dining Out Manners, American and Continental Dining, Appropriate Dress Attire, History of Tea, Types of Tea, Tea Pairings and Tastings, Tea Food Dining Instructions, and Formalities for Preparing a "Proper" Afternoon Tea. This latest volume is an updated compilation of Volume I and Volume II with additional étiquette guidelines and instructions.

The Art of Timeless Étiquette, Graceful Dining Manners, & Afternoon Tea offers practical knowledge in basic social skills for all occasions and settings and includes useful information and advice to enhance one's lifestyle in the social and business world. It takes the reader through a brief history of étiquette, offers introduction methods and conversation techniques, provides guidelines for entertaining, presents illustrations for formal, informal, and family style table settings, and explains the difference between Continental and American style dining. It also provides instructions on the proper way to consume soups, beverages, tea, coffee, and various difficult foods.

With beautiful photographs, exquisite china, gleaming silver, and stunning floral bouquets, *The Art of Timeless Étiquette, Graceful Dining Manners, & Afternoon Tea* delights the senses with elegant and picturesque table settings, antique teacups, and beautiful linens.

In the chapters dedicated to Afternoon Tea, detailed information is provided on the history of tea, styles of tea, types of tea, tea pairings with fruits and savories, and tea tasting characteristics. Instructions are provided on making the perfect pot of tea for this charming custom as it became the forefront of high society. Detailed guidelines are presented on how to set a proper tea table and how to set up a tea style buffet along with instructions on dining with savories, scones, and petits fours.

This newest volume illustrates various methods for conducting oneself gracefully in his or her professional life keeping in mind the importance of first impressions. The chapter on virtues contains important information on self-discipline, friendship, courage, and other aspects for living a good life.

As an added bonus, *The Art of Timeless Étiquette, Graceful Dining Manners, & Afternoon Tea* contains chapters on the history, usage, and care of all tableware that includes flatware, dinnerware, stemware, and crystal. Credit is given to Richard Osterberg's book, *Sterling Silver*

Flatware (Published in 1994 by Schiffer Publishing Ltd.) for much of this information. Mr. Osterberg's continuing and passionate interest in antiques and silver began during his Vermont childhood. He was introduced to a goldsmith and silversmith from Scotland and over time developed an interest in English, Scottish, and American silver which resulted in several publications.

Credit is given to William Hanson who is the leading étiquette coach and social commentator in the United Kingdom. His life's work is and continues to be the training of royalty, government officials, diplomats, and VIPs who wish to integrate good manners into the global forum. Mr. Hanson's expert advice is absolutely priceless.

Whether one is a homemaker, business professional, or student, *The Art of Timeless Étiquette, Graceful Dining Manners, & Afternoon Tea* will empower every reader with confidence as he or she learns life-changing essential manners and practical skills while exploring the world of étiquette.

My mother wouldn't think twice about inviting family and friends over for dinner. She set a lovely table and what made it truly beautiful was her easy spirit of sharing. That is what entertaining is all about.

Étiquette

For many, the word "étiquette" implies white gloves, finger bowls, children curtsying, and other genteel manners that once were the hallmark of proper behavior. The actual definition of étiquette is a system of conventional rules that regulate social behavior. The etymology of this French word literally means a "ticket" or "card" and refers to the bygone custom of a French monarch who instituted ceremonial rules and regulations for members of court. The ticket or card would indicate the proper dress code, expected impeccable behavior, and dining instructions for all who attended court. While these elaborate court rituals have come and gone along with other archaic customs, today's rules of étiquette remain traditional and constant.

Brief History of Étiquette

Since the dawn of time, social skills, manners, and rules have existed so societies could cooperate and survive. In man's early efforts to interact smoothly with others, he created ways to make life easier and more pleasant. In doing so, certain practices developed for all aspects of life. While table manners were probably low on a long list of priorities, the chief focus was on sustenance for survival. Eating implements and utensils evolved mainly out of necessity, not fashion. When fire became a means to cook foods, burned fingers surely led to the employment of sticks, shells, animal bones, and whatever else was handy for bringing the food to one's mouth. Sometimes a stick fastened to a shell allowed for a longer reach or protection from steam if a liquid was hot. Animal horns from sheep and goats also functioned as vessels for liquid. These early utensils did not last very long and were eventually replaced by other suitable items with the development of copper and other malleable materials.

Though evidence shows forks were used throughout early history and during the Roman Empire, the Dark Ages in Europe brought many changes, including the abandonment of forks and spoons for dining. Instead, double-edged knives, fingers, cupped hands, and hollowed-out trenchers (a primitive plate made of dried bread) came into use by the majority of Western Europe. Forks and spoons remained in use in the Middle East and Africa though more commonly for serving purposes. Chopsticks were favored by Asian cultures. Dining with one's hands, however, remained a popular method among the more primitive societies.

Soups and broths were drunk from saucers and bowls. Within time, bread trenchers were replaced by wood, pewter, and porcelain tableware depending on the household and family budget. While eating, pinkie fingers were extended and kept away from the greasy foods so they could be used for dipping into expensive spices.

By 1533, Catherine de Medici of Italy brought several dozen small dining forks with her when she arrived in France to marry Henry II. She was the first notable to have used forks as eating utensils in Western Europe. Considered an oddity at first, the fork slowly became popularized in European courts. Silver utensils of all sorts along with Chinese-inspired tableware were created for the wealthy.

As table manners evolved throughout Europe and with more foods available, larger and more extensive sets of silver were created for the table. By the mid-eighteen hundreds silver electroplating made utensils affordable for the growing middle classes of Europe and America. Silver-plated utensils and sterling dining implements were marketed as "heirlooms of the future." These were the luxury items every household needed and could be passed down to future generations. Every food item soon had its own utensil.

During the Victorian Era, hosts and hostesses became fond of highly specialized and elaborately decorated flatware. Numerous styles of ice-cream forks, corn scrapers, orange spoons, and mango forks were created. Implements were designed specifically for serving olives, peas, baked potatoes, berries, and for tinned fish such as sardines and herring. Bread was served with specifically designed forks. Even crackers had their own scoop-like serving spoons. Pickled foods were served with ornately adorned forks, spears and tongs along with pickle castors.

The finest of dining became an event with silver utensils flanking place settings of beautiful porcelain and crystal. These were the items that separated the wealthy of society from those not so fortunate. The expression, "one knows the correct fork to use," suddenly became synonymous with being well mannered, though one had little to do with the other. It was simply society's way of distinguishing between classes.

The late nineteenth and early twentieth centuries also saw a greater influx of reading material for the everyday homemaker and businessman on how to avoid social faux pas in everyday life. Numerous popular books on étiquette, dress, culture, and decorum came from society mavens and gents determined to spread the word on proper decorum. Books also covered the dyeing of fabrics, grooming tips, color coordination for skin tone, hair color, dress color, and even palm reading—a favorite Victorian pastime for women. Many books included advice on greeting heads of state and European royalty.

By the late nineteen hundreds, society in the presumed "civilized" world began to accept a more relaxed standard of manners which has continued up to today. However, though it is known that invitations require a response and that the appropriateness of one's dress is still a factor in how others view us, modern society still has the need and is still interested when it comes to étiquette and manners. Fortunately, over the years, books have been written on étiquette that encompass not only the acceptable customs from the past but also allow for new customs resulting from the leaps taken in technology and the changes which have taken place.

Introduction Methods

Introducing people is an integral part of good manners. People feel much more at ease after being introduced. Outlined in this chapter are several different introductory methods.

Formal Introductions Present the person who is younger, has less prestige, or is not the guest of honor to the person who is older, has more prestige, or is the guest of honor. Examples: Present your friend to Dr. Birch, "Dr. Birch, I would like you to meet my friend, Christopher." Present your friend to your mother, "Mother, I would like you to meet my friend Robert." Present a woman to a man. It is also customary for men to stand for women. Women may stand if the person introduced to them is older as a mark of respect.

Always address people by Mr., Ms., or Mrs., and their last name.
(Mx. for a non-gendered person).
It is polite to wait and be invited to use a person's first name.

Introducing Yourself It is your job to let others know who you are whether you are in a formal, an informal, or a workplace setting. Often someone else will introduce you, but sometimes it will be left up to you. When it is left up to you, be sure to enunciate clearly, "My name is John Smith. I am pleased to meet you." Or, if this is a work situation, "My name is Jane Smith, Human Relations Manager of Acme Corporation."

Introducing a Number of People When introducing a number of people, clearly state each person's name preferably in the order in which they are standing to avoid confusion. If you are a member of a group being introduced, please nod your head when your name is mentioned and make eye contact with the person being introduced. If you are introducing a group and do not know everyone's name, ask each member of the group to introduce himself or herself.

It can be uncomfortable if one cannot remember a person's name; however, there is nothing wrong with asking someone to refresh your memory by asking his or her name.

Introducing a Spouse It is an outmoded custom to introduce your spouse as Mr. Brown or Mrs. Johnson. It is preferable to say, "This is my husband, Jim." Because many married women today keep their maiden names, you might say, "This is my wife, Catherine James." It is never acceptable to joke your way through an introduction such as, "This is the ball-and-chain," or, "Meet the mister."

Introducing Relatives Make the relationship between you and your relative clear. For example, it is proper to say, "Sharon Clark, I want to introduce Tom Owens, my uncle." Be sure to give the last names.

Handshaking—the Ultimate Greeting Shaking hands creates a favorable impression and influences others to do the same. The handshake is important because it is the accepted greeting in almost all countries. Always shake hands when: introduced to a person and when you say goodbye, when someone comes into your office to see you, when you meet someone outside your office or home, when you enter a room, when you leave a gathering, when you congratulate someone who has won an award or given a speech, and when you are consoling someone. Be sure to make eye contact. Smile while shaking someone's hand. Smiling triggers positive endorphins. A firm but not overpowering handshake is usually a good idea. Be especially careful how much pressure you exert if you are shaking hands with an elderly person or if you are wearing heavy rings that might bruise. Be sure your handshake is both firm and brief. Count to three and let go. Also, use your right hand even if you are left-handed because most people are right-handed.

Always stand when shaking hands and never shake hands over a barrier (desk, etc.). In America, people usually shake hands with two shakes.

Historically, gentlemen would frequently carry swords since they could never be quite sure who their friends were. When engaging in combat, they would unsheathe their weapons using their right hand as the sword was carried in a scabbard on their left hip. Therefore, when meeting someone they considered a friend, they would show that they meant no harm by presenting their right hand away from the left hip, palm open, to confirm they were not holding a weapon.

Removing Gloves Remove your gloves before you shake a person's hand. Unless there is a reason not to, it is best to remove your gloves as soon as you arrive at an event.

Gloves are often thought of as something born of the Napoleonic era. In fact, gloves have been worn for over ten thousand years. Of course, the earliest uses were not for fashion but were more utilitarian in purpose. Gloves protected one's hands from harsh weather or hard labor. Even thousands of years ago, gloves were not worn during dinner service. This is understandable when you consider that until the sixteen hundreds, food was traditionally eaten with one's fingers.

The Art of Conversation

Stimulating conversation is considered an art. Learning to express thoughts and opinions diplomatically may either come naturally or may need to be developed over time. Effective delivery will allow people to enjoy a conversation with you. The best conversations are calm and quiet interchanging of sentiments where there is no competition and no vanity.

The following questions are conversation starters:

How is the weather?
Who is your favorite entertainer?
Who is your favorite actor?
How do you spend your free time?
Do you have any pets? What are their names?
Have you taken any vacations lately?
What would be your perfect weekend?
Do you enjoy the theatre?
Do you have any cultural pursuits?
What are your personal interests?
Have you read any good books lately?
Are you very active or do you prefer to just relax in your free time?

The following topics should never be included in public conversation:

Any part of a person's body, hair, hair color, or disability
Money
Politics
Religion
Sex
Family
Love life

Entertain with color, composition, and texture. These are the important building blocks for creating a breathtaking table.

Easy Entertaining

ntertaining is one of the greatest gifts bestowed upon people while creating memorable events for family and friends. It is a time for enjoying cherished friends, introducing family members to old friends, and creating an atmosphere that is warm and welcoming. One of the most welcoming aspects of entertaining is to create a beautiful table that will add brilliance and peacefulness to a meal. Mixing antique collections with contemporary pieces adds drama and a sense of the unexpected whether setting a formal, an informal, or a family table setting.

Hopefully, this chapter will inspire hosts and hostesses to entertain and also inspire guests to be entertained in the most elegant fashion. Above all, graciousness should be the most outstanding characteristic for all.

The first step to entertaining begins with sending out invitations. Invitations are very important and should be designed or purchased to fit the occasion. There is a lot of flexibility and variation to style, paper, color, and wording. There is also proper protocol for addressing individuals.

Invitations When hosting an extremely formal dinner party or any other formal social function, it is recommended to have your invitations engraved. Include the name of the host or hostess, date, time, and location. Include the person being honored or the event celebrated. Include the preferred dress code—for example: black tie, white tie, or business casual, etc. If the event is a formal dinner party, inform your guests as to exactly when the dinner will be served to avoid inadvertent tardiness. This may be done in the following British manner: "Please come at 7:30 PM for cocktails. Dinner will be served at 8:00 PM." This allows nondrinkers to come at the end of the cocktail period to avoid any kind of awkwardness.

Invitations are written in third person: "Mr. and Mrs. John Smith invite you to dinner…" Let your guests know whom you are honoring in the invitation. Include a map, especially if the event is in a hard-to-find location.

Sending Formal Invitations by Post Send engraved or handwritten formal invitations out three to six weeks before the date of the event. This may vary by situation and purpose. In a large metropolis where there is a busy social scene, invitations must be sent out early. Formal balls, weddings, and fundraising events are often announced up to three months in advance.

Sending Informal Invitations by Post Send informal invitations out at least two weeks in advance. Invitations may be purchased at a stationery store. A variety of fill-in cards are available, less expensive, and quite practical. There is much more flexibility and variation as to the style and paper color of these invitations.

If you do not hear from someone to whom you have sent a written invitation, do not hesitate to call the person. However, do it in a non-accusatory way. Do not say, "I've been waiting to hear from you," which implies the invitee has been rude to keep you waiting. It is much more gracious to call and say, "I'm so sorry, but I seem to have mislaid your acceptance card. Could you remind me whether you are coming?"

Reminder Cards Send reminder cards to arrive approximately ten days before the scheduled event. The traditional reminder card is an engraved fill-in card. If you wish to be less formal, use your personal stationery to write the reminder.

If hosting an impromptu gathering, you may do the inviting by telephone, particularly when it is less than two weeks away.

Receiving an Invitation When you receive an invitation by personal letter, reply by letter. When the R.s.v.p. provides a telephone number, reply by telephone.

If children are not included by name in the invitation, or unless the invitation specifically says, "Mr. and Mrs. Joe Brown and Family," children are not invited. Do not bring them or put the host or hostess in an awkward position by asking if they may come. If children are not invited, there is probably a good reason, whether it is financial, social, or simply a case of an inappropriate scene for non-adults.

Uninvited Guests or Pets When you are invited to a formal dinner, a wedding, or even an informal party, it is not acceptable to bring along uninvited guests. If you are single and the invitation reads "Mr. So and So and Guest" or "Ms. Whoever and Escort," you are well within your social bounds to bring one guest. It is impolite to call the host or hostess to ask if you may bring additional guests. The exceptions to this rule are the following: a) you have recently become engaged or married, b) you will be entertaining a house guest from out of town, or c) you require the need of a service dog.

Leaving an Event Early Inform the host or hostess when you arrive at the event that you are leaving at a certain time. When the time comes to leave, discretely remind the host or hostess, express your thanks, and quietly leave. You leave quietly so as not to take any attention away from the guest of honor or to break up the flow of the event (opening gifts/eating). Remember to send a thank-you note to the host or hostess the next day.

Sample Engraved Dinner Invitation

Mr. and Mrs. John Smith

request the pleasure of your company
at *Christmas Dinner*
on *Saturday, the twenty-fourth of December*
at *seven o'clock*
430 Jefferson Street

R.s.v.p. 360.999.9999
430 Jefferson Street
Langley, Washington 91234

R.s.v.p. literally means "Répondez S'il Vous Plaît" (translation: Please Respond). This French phrase on an invitation indicates you must respond with your intent either to attend or not to attend. Many people believe if they are not going to attend, they may disregard the invitation. However, this means the host or hostess will not know until the last minute how many people he or she will be serving.

Salutations and Subscriptions

Married woman who takes husband's name:
    Mrs. Joe Smith

Married woman keeping maiden name:
    Ms. Michelle Jones

Hyphenated name:
    Ms. Michelle Jones-Smith

Widow:
    Mrs. Joe Smith

Divorced woman:
    Mrs. Michelle Smith

Boys under the age of 12:
    Master Tommy Tinker or Masters Tommy Tinker and Brian Tinker

Plural for Mr. is Messrs.:
    Messrs. Mark Jones and John Smith

Girls remain Miss until they marry:
    Miss Julie Smith

Two people married with different names:
    Mr. William Jones and Ms. Amy Williams

Historically, the reason a woman takes a man's name is because when she becomes a bride and walks down the aisle, her father gives her away to another man who now owns her.

Salutations and Subscriptions

Salutation: Dear Sir,
Dear Madam,
To whom it may concern,
Subscription: Yours faithfully,

Salutation: Dear Mr. Henderson,
Subscription: Yours sincerely,

Salutation: Dear Stephen,
Subscription: Yours ever,

Salutation: Dear William,
Subscription: With all good wishes,
With very warm wishes and thanks,

Flamboyant ways to sign off with close friends:
All love and hugs,
Yours affectionately,
The quaintest of quaints,
Love, love, love,

Honorifics (Signing off)

Bernadette M. Petrotta
William Jones

One never gives his or her own person respect with a Ms., Mrs., or Mr. Other people can address you with Ms., Mrs., or Mr.—not you yourself!

Mx. is used to address a non-gendered person.

Historically, a person's surname was not considered all that important. In early medieval England, most people were known only by one name, their "Christian name," such as Thomas or Anne, which was conferred at baptism. But as the population grew, it got tiresome trying to distinguish among the many Thomases or Annes, so surnames arose, often based on lineage (such as Williamson), occupation (such as Smith), or locale (such as York).

However, the matter of a wife taking a husband's surname didn't surface in English common law until the ninth century when lawmakers began to consider the legalities surrounding personhood, families, and marriage. Thusly (as they would say), the doctrine of coverture emerged—and women thereafter were considered "one" with their husbands and therefore required to assume the husband's surname as their own.

Under the concept of coverture, which literally means "covered by," women had no independent legal identity apart from their spouse. This "coverage" began upon the birth of a female baby—who was given her father's surname—and could only change upon the marriage of that female, at which point her name was automatically changed to that of her new husband.

But coverture laws also prevented women from entering into contracts, engaging in litigation, participating in business, or exercising ownership over real estate or personal property. As succinctly stated by former Justice Abe Fortas of the United States Supreme Court in United States v. Yazell, "(c)overture…rests on the old common-law fiction that the husband and wife are one, [and] the one is the husband."

In the seventeenth- and eighteenth-century France, the bourgeoisie—the middle class—were far stricter about manners than the nobility. As there was no king standing nearby to enforce the rules of étiquette, the bourgeoisie saw it as up to them to impose and dictate the rules of civility, which meant they could be considered even worse snobs than their more prestigious counterparts.

Set a beautiful table with new and old family pieces. Create a regal and elegant ambience by taking a little extra time to set a table with smart cutlery, bone china, and stemware that will invite a sense of occasion to any formal dinner or weekend brunch.

Formal Seated Dinner with a Staff Entertaining formally can be a delightful experience if it is served by a properly schooled staff that is well-trained, efficient, and includes an accomplished chef. Even though the easiest way to give such a dinner is in a hotel or a club, the intimacy and the uniqueness of having a dinner in your own home may be very rewarding. Preparations made well in advance make for a more relaxed host and hostess. One of the key elements of any dinner party is the guest list. Guests should be compatible.

As guests arrive, the host or hostess and guest or guests of honor should be at the entrance so introductions may be made upon entering.

Before dinner service is announced, guests are expected to circulate and meet other guests. This often includes cocktails or other refreshments in the drawing room (living room). When the butler announces dinner is ready, the host should take the female guest of honor and the hostess should take the male guest of honor and both should lead the procession into the dining area. Each gentleman seats the woman that will be sitting on his right and remains standing until the hostess is ready to sit down.

When dinner service is announced, drinks should be left in the drawing room and not taken to the dining table.

Traditionally at a formal dinner, the host sits at the head of the table with the hostess at the other end. This works whenever there are six, ten, fourteen, or eighteen guests. However, when the number of guests is divisible by four, it is not possible for the hostess to sit at the end of the table. In this case, the hostess moves one place to the left, with the man on her right sitting at the end of the table, opposite the host. This will keep the tradition of seating guests male, female, male, female, etc. Husbands and wives are never seated next to each other.

Historically, a drawing room represented a formal space that was mainly used for entertaining guests. Around the seventeenth century, after dinner, men assembled for wine and cigars or just lingered on in the same room where dinner was served. The women would "withdraw" to a different room called the "withdrawing room." Somehow the name shortened to "drawing room." In modern times, a living room is often found at the center of the house and is generally furnished with comfortable chairs, sofas, recliners, a television, etc. In today's homes, a living room usually takes the place of a drawing room.

In the early twentieth century it was expected that no female guest would enter the dining room alone. According to tradition, a woman needed a man to "guide" her. Thus, after the butler formally announced "Dinner is served" to the waiting guests, each male guest—having already been informed of his partner—would offer his arm to a woman and guide her to her chair. The host would enter first, himself being partnered with the most esteemed and senior woman guest. Then the other paired guests would follow, according to the woman's rank, with the hostess entering and sitting last, the senior male guest on her arm.

Formal Table Seating for Six, Ten, Fourteen, or Eighteen People

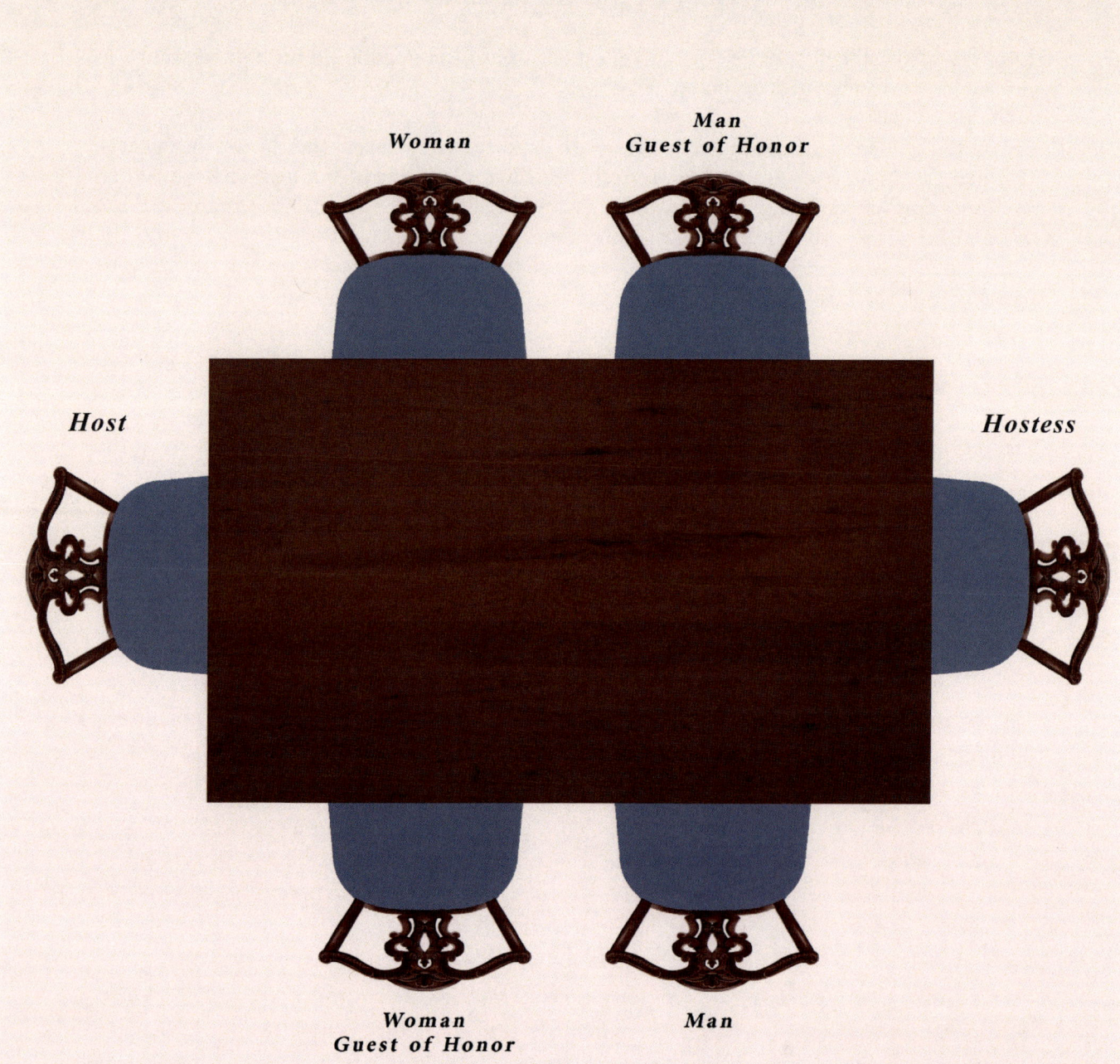

16

Formal Table Seating for Groups Divisible by Four

In a formal seated dinner, the butler is positioned behind the hostess if he is not otherwise engaged. He should not leave the dining room. His purpose is to supervise the other employees. Seldom does he serve the food, and if he does, it is the main course. He may also be in charge of opening and pouring wine.

The hostess will place a napkin on her lap. Guests should follow suit.

When it comes to serving the food, the female guest of honor always is served first. The basic rule is to serve the female guest of honor and continue to serve in a counterclockwise manner until all the guests are served. The host is, therefore, served last.

Once the food has been served, everyone waits to eat until the hostess picks up her fork, unless she pointedly encourages her guests to begin eating as soon as their food is served. Also, unless the hostess indicates, one should not even sip a beverage. If there is no hostess, look to the host for a cue.

Order of Courses for Formal Seated Dinner with a Staff

Before dinner – Apéritifs and hors d'œuvres served in the drawing room

Dinner: Appetizer (Entrée)
          Soup – Sherry
          Fish Course – White Wine
          Meat/Fowl Course – Red Wine
          Salad
          Fruit/Cheese
          Dessert – Champagne

After dinner – Digestifs (port and brandy) served in the dining room (men)

After dinner – Coffee, tea, and liqueurs served in the drawing room (women)

The English serve pudding before the fruit/cheese course as part of the main meal. Pudding comes from the French word boudin. Dessert is a separate course that follows the pudding. Meals were much longer and stodgier back in the Victorian days and so a piece of fruit was served on a plate to act as a palate cleanser. At this stage the tablecloths were often drawn or at the very best the wine glasses and any leftover cutlery and crockery were taken away if the cloths were to be left. This was "dessert," as it was served after everything had been cleared from the table. The word dessert comes from the French word desservir.

The term canapé comes from the French word for "couch." This makes sense if you look at the garnish as a person, sitting on a couch. Nonetheless, it is expected that a canapé be salty or spicy, as its job as an hors d'œuvres is to increase the guests' appetites.

Dishes should not be cleared until all guests have finished their meal. Once the table is cleared after each course (appetizer, soup, fish, meat/fowl, salad), fruit and cheese are often served followed by dessert. At the completion of dessert, the hostess should place her napkin on the table to signal dinner is over. She should then invite the women to retire to the drawing room for coffee, tea, and liqueurs. The men often stay in the dining room for port and brandy. The host may ask the men whether they want to enjoy coffee, tea, and liqueurs in the drawing room with the women. Sometimes the conversation at the dining table is so stimulating and spirited, the hostess may decide not to break up the conversation and serve coffee, tea, and liqueurs in the dining room. In this case, the butler should be alerted to the change of plans.

*Flowers are the jewels we can all enjoy.
Bring them into your home and your life.
Indulge your passion with a touch of refinement.*

Formal Seated Dining Table Setting with a Staff Set the table with a white linen tablecloth and allow it to hang over the edge of the table by twelve inches or more. Napkins should match the tablecloth and should be placed in the center of each charger. The most elegant and exquisite china, flatware, and stemware should be utilized. The patterns do not have to be the same for the entire dinner but should be similar within each course.

Set stemware is in a semicircle, beginning with a sherry glass for the soup course, a white wine glass for the fish course, a claret or burgundy glass for the meat course, a water goblet for water to rinse the palate, followed by a champagne glass for the dessert. Port and brandy stemware should be added later.

Traditionally, in front of each guest or between two guests, a salt cellar is set with its own spoon and a pepper pot.

In some formal dinners, the host or hostess may want to serve dessert in the drawing room. In this case, the dessert utensils should not be set in the initial setting as shown in the following diagram.

Since coffee, tea, and liqueurs are served in the drawing room, all stemware, cups, and saucers should not be set on the table in the initial setting. They should be brought separately into the drawing room after dinner by the staff.

All plates should be round—not square.

Service à la française versus service à la russe: The Russian Prince Kourakin was credited, in the 1830s in Paris, with first introducing service à la russe. Félex Urbain Dubois, who served as chef to Prince Orloff in Russia, did a great deal to popularize the "Russian" method of service when he returned to Paris in the 1870s. In service à la russe courses were brought to each diner sequentially on plates held by servants. In contrast, service à la française offered a feast for the eyes as well as the appetite. It offered a broad and immediate choice since all of the dishes, candles, and elaborate centerpieces were laid on the table. Diners helped themselves from the serving dishes.

An early complaint about service à la russe was that owners of enormous numbers of serving dishes were no longer able to display all of their silver and valuable porcelain as they did with service à la française.

Formal Seated Dining Table Setting with a Staff

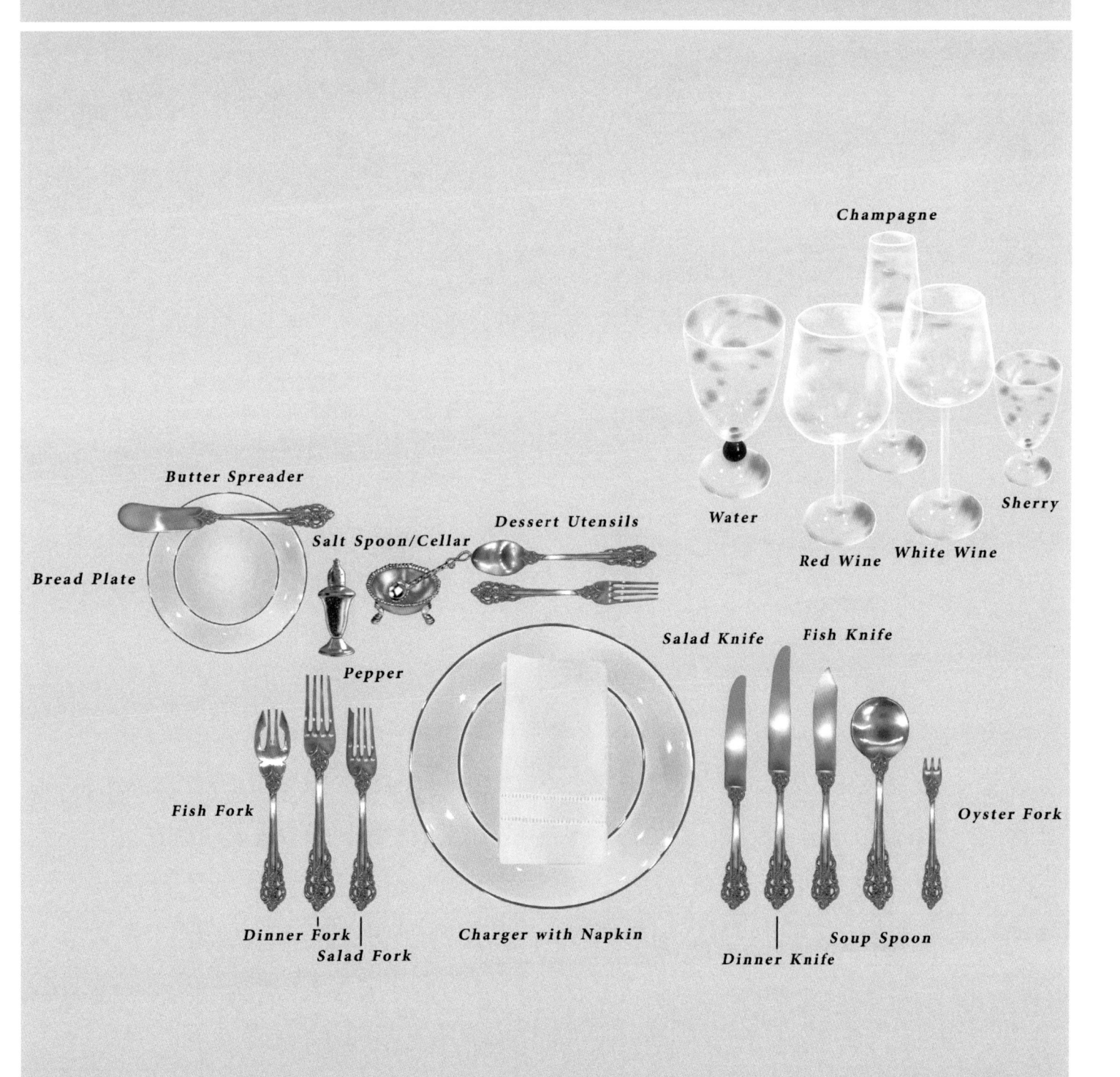

Champagne

Butter Spreader

Dessert Utensils — Water

Salt Spoon/Cellar

Sherry

Bread Plate

Red Wine — White Wine

Pepper

Salad Knife — Fish Knife

Fish Fork

Oyster Fork

Dinner Fork | Charger with Napkin | Soup Spoon
Salad Fork — Dinner Knife

21

Historically, the word "dinner" refers to the first meal of a two-meal day—a heavy meal occurring about noon, which broke the night's fast into the new day. The word is from the French word disner—meaning "to dine" from the stem of the word désjunare ("to break one's fast").

The first Pilgrim settlers still thought of England as "home." Though they had come to America to worship in their own way, they weren't planning to create a new country. They still wanted to be English and when they told their children to be good, they meant to be like the English children.

But the Pilgrim's manners weren't always the same as ours. In their first years in America, they were often too busy for regular meals. People just helped themselves right out of the cooking pot. They ate standing—in front of the fire, especially if the day was cold—and then hurried back to work again.

When the family did eat together, the dinner table was often just some old boards laid on top of barrels. The cooking pot simply was placed in the middle and the family gathered around.

Later, when the Pilgrims had more time—and more dishes—food was brought to the table on large round platters called chargers.

No one had his or her own plate. Instead, two people would share a trencher—a bowl carved or burned out of a block of wood.

All parents and children shared trenchers. The Pilgrims thought that people who had their own trenchers were show-offs.

Some poor people didn't have these wooden trenchers. Instead, they used pieces of stale bread as plates. They put the food on top. After they had eaten the food, they ate the bread plates as well.

Almost nobody used a fork. One Pilgrim, Governor John Winthrop, was given a fork as a present. It had only two tines. The Pilgrims called it a "double dagger." But everyone needed a spoon because the Pilgrims ate plenty of soups and stews. The first spoons made in Plymouth were clamshells attached to sticks. Buffalo horns made good spoons, too. Later, when they had more time, people carved spoons out of wood. Some lucky folks had brought pewter or silver spoons from England.

Everyone had his or her own knife. If you were a grown-up, it was acceptable to stick your knife right into the pot and pull out a piece of food. But children were not to take any food for themselves; they were supposed to eat whatever their parents handed to them.

It was always fine to eat with your fingers. The only rule was that you were to wash them or at least wipe them before you stuck them in the pot.

Naturally, this meant that everyone needed a very large napkin. The Pilgrims threw the napkin over one shoulder or tied it around their necks. The napkin hung down almost to their knees. You could also use it to grab pieces of hot food.

Beautiful and ornate flatware make for an elegant table. Enjoy the diversity of patterns and history each piece entails.

Informal Seated Dinner without a Staff Hosting an informal dinner without a staff is one of the most popular ways to entertain. As host or hostess, one must be very organized and willing to cook, bartend, serve, and clean up. Meals should be planned well ahead to avoid last minute preparations.

As guests arrive, the host or hostess and guest or guests of honor should be at the entrance so introductions may be made upon entering.

Before dinner service is announced, guests are expected to circulate and meet other guests. This often includes cocktails or other refreshments in the drawing room. When dinner is ready, the hostess should make the announcement. She should then, along with the host, take the guest or guests of honor into the dining area. Each gentleman seats the woman who will be sitting on his right and should remain standing until the hostess is ready to sit down. When dinner service is announced, unlike formal dining, drinks may be taken into the dining room.

Seating at an informal dinner is identical to seating at a formal dinner. The host sits at the head of the table with the hostess at the other end. Again, this works whenever there are six, ten, fourteen, or eighteen guests. However, when the number of guests is divisible by four, it is not possible for the hostess to sit at the end of the table. In this case, like the formal dinner, the hostess moves one place to the left, with the man on her right sitting at the end of the table, opposite the host, thus keeping the guests alternating male and female.

The host and hostess might begin dinner with soup, an appetizer such as melon, or a shellfish (oyster) cocktail. This first course should be on each guest's charger right before each guest enters the dining room. Therefore, the table should be set accordingly. If the first course is soup, the table should be set with a soup spoon placed on the right side of the knives; if the first course is melon, the table should be set with a teaspoon placed on the right side of the knives; if the first course is an oyster cocktail, the table should be set with an oyster fork placed on the right side of the knives.

After this first course is finished, all dishes should be removed. Clean salad dishes should be set. Rolls and salad are brought in separately for the guests to pass to one another. When the salad course is finished, salad dishes along with the chargers should be taken into the kitchen and the main course should be prepared. The most practical way to serve the main course without help is to fill the dinner plates in the kitchen and serve them to the guests two at a time. The host and hostess may also decide to serve the main course at the table. In this case, the host usually serves the food. After all of the guests have been served, the food is taken to the kitchen to be kept hot until seconds are offered.

Since hosting an informal dinner may be served several ways, try to keep in mind to serve beginning with the female guest of honor or the female to the host's right and continuing counterclockwise and ending with the host. Remember, once the food has been served, everyone waits to eat until the hostess picks up her fork, unless she pointedly encourages her guests to begin eating when their food is served. If there is no hostess, look to the host for a cue.

As with a formal dinner, flatware at a place setting is used from the outside in, toward the dinner plate, as each course is served.

Also, as with formal dinners, the host or hostess may want to serve dessert in the drawing room. In this case, the dessert utensils should not be set in the initial setting as shown in the following diagram.

Since coffee, tea, and liqueurs are served in the drawing room, all stemware, cups, and saucers should not be set on the table in the initial setting. They should be brought separately to the drawing room when needed.

Informal Seated Dining Table Setting without a Staff

Butter Spreader

Salt Spoon/Cellar   Dessert Utensils   Water

Pepper   Wine

Bread Plate   Salad Knife

Oyster Fork

Napkin   Dinner Fork
Salad Fork   Charger with Appetizer/Entrée   Dinner Knife

Family Style Dining When entertaining family style and have prepared the food, it is acceptable to serve the salad with the rest of the food rather than as a separate course. Remember, serving family style is just as important as "formal or informal" dining and one should use the nicest tableware. All family members should observe the dinner hour. This is a good time to instruct dining methods such as American or Continental and how to eat difficult foods. All members of the family should follow simple dining étiquette such as putting their napkin on their lap, not talking with food in their mouth, and waiting for everyone to sit down before eating. There should be no gossiping at the table or answering the telephone during dinner.

Family Style Dining Table Setting The following page depicts a typical table setting for everyday use in the home. The dinner plate should be placed in the middle of the setting, the salad plate to the left of the forks, and the napkin to the left of the salad plate—never on the dinner plate.

After all diners have finished, everything should be removed from the table.

If serving fruit, cheese, or nuts, treat them as separate courses. Dessert is also a separate course served with its own plates and flatware. Coffee, tea, and liqueurs may be served with dessert or in the drawing room after dessert.

Family Style Dining Table Setting

Butter Spreader

Bread Plate

Water

Napkin   **Salad Plate**   *Dinner Fork*   **Dinner Plate**   **Dinner Knife**
Salad Fork   *Soup Spoon*

Classic Style Buffet Dining Buffet means "sideboard" in French. Basically, the word buffet has more than one meaning. In one sense it is a piece of furniture used for placing food upon. Another meaning for the word buffet is a variety of cold and hot savory dishes. In classic style buffet dining, the host or hostess should place the food courses on the buffet along with dinner plates, flatware, stemware, and napkins. Dinner plates are placed on the opposite side of flatware, stemware, and napkins. The food courses are placed in the middle of the buffet. The host or hostess may help serve their guests, or guests may serve themselves. Ladies are served first. As soon as the guests are served or have served themselves from the buffet, they should find a comfortable place to sit and eat. Guests do not need to wait for everyone to be served in order to begin eating. The host and hostess serve themselves last.

Flowers, candles, or other decorations may be placed on the buffet provided there is sufficient room.

Coffee, tea, liqueurs, stemware, cups, and saucers along with dessert plates and dessert utensils are placed on a separate table. An additional table should be included for used plates.

Beautiful silver to adorn your table.

Classic Style Buffet Setting

Dinner Plates

Sit-Down Style Buffet Dining Sit-down style buffet dining is more formal than classic style buffet dining. The host or hostess should place the food courses on the buffet along with the dinner plates only. Warm dinner plates may be set on a trivet. The dining table should be set in the usual way with the exception of the dinner plates. This, of course, is the most comfortable way to dine buffet style. Again, the host or hostess may help serve their guests, or guests may serve themselves. Ladies are served first. After the guests are served or have served themselves from the buffet, they should take their seats at the dining table. The hostess should guide her guests as to where to sit or she may have put place cards on the table. As in the classic style buffet, the host and hostess serve themselves last.

Coffee, tea, liqueurs, stemware, cups, and saucers along with dessert plates and dessert utensils are placed on a separate table. An additional table should be included for used plates.

As previously mentioned, a sideboard is furniture used in the dining room for serving food. It usually consists of a set of cabinets, or cupboards, and one or more drawers. The overall height is approximately waist level. The earliest versions of the sideboard made their appearance in the eighteenth century but gained most of their popularity during the nineteenth century as households became prosperous enough to dedicate a room solely to dining.

Sit-Down Style Buffet Setting

Dinner Plates

Sit-Down Style Buffet Dining Table Setting

Table "crumbers" or scrapers are used by the butler, host, or hostess after the main course prior to the dessert or fruit course. Crumbers may be miniature brooms or brushes with small or long handles.

Candles add atmosphere and ambiance to table settings. Candle étiquette dictates curtains should be drawn when candles are lighted.

Additional Entertaining Guidelines

* When setting the table, a pad should be placed under the tablecloth to protect it against spills. For formal table settings, the tablecloth should hang over the edge of the table by twelve inches or more. For less formal table settings, the tablecloth should hang over the edge of the table by eight inches.

* As shown in the picture on the previous page, candles add atmosphere and ambience. Candle étiquette dictates curtains are drawn when candles are lighted.

* The day before a dinner, ice should be ordered, tablecloths and napkins should be pressed, and table and bar area should be set. After dinner, tea, coffee, and liqueur trays ought to be arranged and furniture positioned to suit guests. Set coasters on tables where needed and set hand-written place cards.

* Place cards are arranged by the host or hostess. Guests should never tamper with their position. Place cards serve many purposes. The card indicates a person's name and is used to mark his or her place at the dining table. A tent-style place card is positioned above each person's dinner plate or charger. A flat card is placed on the charger.

* Party favors or table favors are quite entertaining. The host or hostess will encourage guests as to when favors should be opened.

* Cheese is very popular and there is a proper way for it to be served. Guests may help themselves without assistance from the host or hostess. Cheese should be served at room temperature along with serving utensils such as proper cheese knives and proper cheese spoons. An example of a proper cheese spoon is a Stilton spoon. At least three hors d'œuvres—hot or cold—depending on the season should be served.

* Wine and champagne stemware are filled a little over halfway without lifting the stemware from the table. To prevent dripping, the neck of the bottle should be gently lifted away from the mouth of the stemware—in a circular motion. A napkin should be wrapped loosely around the neck of a champagne or wine bottle with the label exposed.

* When serving apéritifs at cocktail hour, fill stemware about one-third.

* Red wine should be served room temperature and white wine should be served gently chilled.

* There is so much flexibility when serving alcoholic beverages. However, wine and food should complement each other. It is preferable to serve lighter wines before heavier wines. The general guidelines recommend white wines before red wines and red wines before sweet dessert wines.

* Stemware may stay in place throughout the meal or be removed after a particular wine is no longer being served.

* If butter is set on the table, it should be rolled into small balls or molded into flower shapes or other interesting shapes.

* Chargers are sometimes referred to as place plates. They are larger than dinner plates. They are set on the table at the beginning of the meal and should not be removed until dinner is served.

* Service plates are known as liners and are placed under cups, soup plates, or even dessert bowls. They are usually small plates in which eating utensils may be placed.

* Rules when using chargers (place plates): Chargers should be set in front of each guest in the initial setting. They are utilized to set service plates, rimmed soup plates, or stemmed glasses which are used for cocktails, soups, or various appetizers. After foods have been consumed, remove all the plates, bowls, and chargers. Following the removal, usually heated dinner plates are placed in front of each guest for the fish course or for the main course (The only time during a dinner when there is no plate in front of a guest is just before the dessert is served).

* When setting the table, the only spoons (soup spoons, melon spoons, or pudding spoons) placed on the right side of chargers or place plates are for soup, melon, pudding or other appetizers. Also, the only forks placed on the right side of chargers are for seafood cocktails or other appetizers.

* In the initial place setting, it is not appropriate to set more than three forks or three knives on either side of chargers or dinner plates.

* Salt and pepper are passed as a pair.

* The bread knife, if set in the initial setting, should be on the right-hand side of the place setting. Traditionally, it would have been the outermost knife on the right-hand side of the place setting and then moved to the bread plate. The butter spreader should be set on the bread plate in the initial setting.

* Demitasse cups are the appropriate cups for after-dinner coffee.

* Flatware, stemware, cups, and saucers are always carried on a tray. For safety and to prevent clattering, the tray should be covered with a napkin.

* Extra napkins should be set in all areas of dining.

* Finger bowls, if using them, should be given to each guest before the fruit course. Each bowl should be filled with room temperature water. A flower blossom may be put in each bowl for decorative purposes. Guests dip their fingers lightly into the water, one hand at a time, and dry them on their napkin.

* American style dining dictates food is served on the <u>left</u> and removed from the <u>right</u>. Continental (European) style dining dictates food is served on the <u>right</u> and removed from the <u>right</u>. United Kingdom (Britain) style dining dictates food is served on the <u>left</u> and removed from the <u>left</u>. Drinks are served and removed on the <u>right</u>. Remember these are only generalizations; serving and removing should not interrupt conversation and must be done as unobtrusively as possible.

* Toasts are festive and seldom out of place. Usually, the first toast is proposed by the host, but not until after the main course has been consumed and cleared. The host stands and gives the toast. If there is a guest of honor, the first toast should be in his or her honor. A hostess may also propose the first toast. The person receiving the toast does not stand or drink when others are raising their stemware to him or her. To do so would be to drink to oneself. He or she should acknowledge the toast by an approving gesture and a "thank you." He or she may respond to the toast immediately or wait for another course of the dinner to be served. In either case, the gracious honoree should stand and say a few words in response.

* People who abstain from alcohol should not raise a glass of water to join in the toast. If they are drinking sparkling cider or soda, they may join in the toast. If not, they should gesture with their hand and arm as though they are holding a glass of wine.

* For women only: Many women instinctively reach for their lipstick at the end of a meal. Please resist and wait until the hostess or host has signaled the meal is over. This is the time to retire to the powder room and refresh your face.

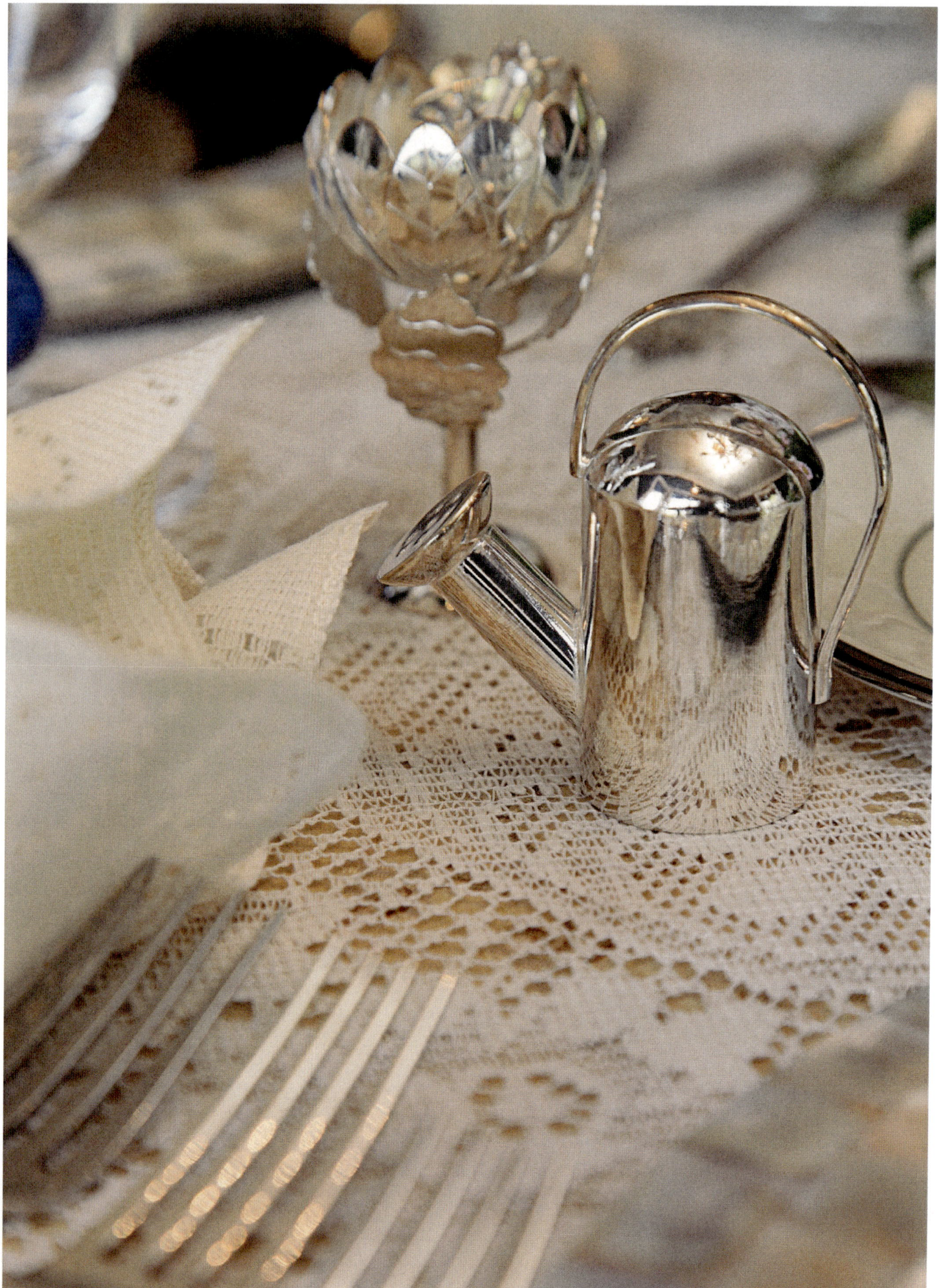

Catherine de Medici is credited with introducing many food innovations to France. She's said to have taught the French how to eat with a fork and introduced foods and dishes such as artichokes, aspics, baby peas, broccoli, cakes, candied vegetables, cream puffs, custards, ices, lettuce, milk-fed veal, melon seeds, parsley, pasta, puff pastry, quenelles, scaloppine, sherbet, sweetbreads, truffles, and zabaglione. She is reputed to have arrived in France with her own personal cooks, pastry chefs, confectioners, and distillers.

On a good day, she's even said to have invented women's knickers.

The essence of hospitality means leaving no detail unattended. Set your table with a sense of poise and a sense of welcome that brings warmth into your home.

Gracious Dining with Flowers, Beautiful Table Settings, and Fine Linens

Flowers add a beautiful touch when setting a table. They bring an uplifting connection with the seasons. Time should be taken to have a flower arrangement made with specific colors depending on the season. If one is fortunate to have a bountiful garden full of fresh flowers, a fresh arrangement will add a sense of style to the table and guests will marvel at the sight.

Beautiful china is always charming for guests or family to see when they enter the dining room. No matter what the occasion, setting an elegant table makes people feel very special. Selecting the right dinner plates and coordinating the mix of patterns is a pleasurable experience. Remember to always hand wash fine china with non-abrasive mild detergent in warm water.

Stemware may be plain or patterned, clear or colored with difference shapes. The shape can affect the taste of the beverage it holds. A basic suite of stemware should include water goblets, champagne flutes, and red and white wine glasses. Crystal stemware is never placed in the dishwasher; it scratches easily.

Flatware says much about the look and design of one's table as much as the choice of china. Some experts think one should choose their flatware pattern first then choose their china and stemware patterns. Sterling silver remains the standard for the finest flatware, but one may also find beautiful silver plate. It is less expensive and may become heirlooms of real quality as well. Both sterling and silver plate should be stored in airtight chests and individually wrapped in tarnish-resistance cloths.

Fine linens are simply an endless parade of colors, textures, and patterns that dress up a table. Whether one chooses lace, linen, or damask in rich colors or pale colors, the ensemble should have tablecloths, table runners, placemats, and dinner and luncheon napkins along with coordinating napkin rings. For more formal settings, one should use white or cream linens. Launder linens by washing and pressing them before storing.

Utilize all of precious items from one's table wardrobe as often as possible.

Alfresco Entertaining

The charm of a relaxed meal or cocktail on the terrace or under an old shade tree sounds extremely inviting. Perhaps there is a corner of the yard that could lend itself to a gathering. If roses are blooming and the butterflies are visiting, one should take advantage of the possibilities. The Italians have a passion for long, leisurely meals and spirited conversation that dates back to the sixteenth century. They have been perfecting outdoor dining for ages.

For a relaxed setting, the table should be set with a cloth and some flowers. Flowers may be arranged in a watering can or a vintage milk bottle. A parade of heirloom tomatoes might be lined up along the center of the table. Table linens do not have to be starched or pressed. The table should be set with casual dinnerware and etched goblets.

For a more whimsical look, perhaps the table should be set with fluted stemware and covered serving pieces with fanciful handles. Dress the table with gingham-checked fabric and top it with beautiful pitchers. The beauty of this kind of tableware goes together effortlessly and dresses up a simple table setting.

The charm of a relaxed meal is the key to happiness and contentment, and most of all brings joy to entertaining.

Celebrate life's milestones and everyday wonders. Create an atmosphere as extraordinary as the menu. Toss white rose petals over the table. Enjoy anniversaries, birthdays, holidays, a dinner for two, or just a luncheon for an old friend.

Before the invention of stainless steel in the 1920s, the taste of blade metal was often said to ruin the flavor of fish. Special silver and silver plate fish knives were invented in the nineteenth century. Before knives, fish was eaten with a fork in the right hand and a piece of bread, as a pusher, held in the left. Two forks were used to serve it and sometimes to eat it as well. Eating fish with forks long remained the choice of the aristocracy.

Flatware

Historically, precious metals have always connoted wealth, and silver flatware was a way to display affluence. Large floor chests were used to store flatware and other sizable silver pieces. A very heavy safe door would protect all these treasures; and when it was bolted and locked, the under butler would sleep with the key beneath his pillow. In some areas years ago, an under butler's bed was the sort that pulled down out of a cupboard and stretched completely across the safe door so it would be impossible for a burglar to get to the safe without awakening the butler.

People frequently employ the term "silverware" to mean all utensils used for eating, but the correct word is "flatware," which encompasses all kinds of metal—sterling, silver plate, and stainless steel. Flatware is the collective name for spoons and forks made by a silversmith. In England the word "cutlery" is used. A "cutler" by tradition fixed a blade to a handle to make scythes, hunting knives, eating knives, and so on.

Sterling Sterling silver is made of 92.5 percent pure silver and 7.5 percent of a base metal, usually copper. Sterling is not one hundred percent silver since silver is too soft for practical purposes and must be alloyed with other metals to give it the strength and hardness necessary for use. Sterling is the most appropriate to use at formal dinners.

Silver Plate Silver plate is made by electroplating a layer of silver to a base metal—usually an alloy of nickel, copper, and zinc. A bar of base metal is dipped into a big tub of water; silver bars are added, then acid, and an electric current is passed through which ionizes the silver molecules. Silver plate may be used at formal dinners.

Stainless Steel An alloy of three metals (chromium, nickel, and steel), stainless steel was born in the twentieth century—a product of the rapidly advancing technology that came out of World War II. Stainless means without stain—it will only stain under extreme conditions. The highest quality stainless steel is marked 18/10—which means eighteen percent chromium and ten percent nickel have been added to the basic steel alloy. Stainless steel is never used at formal settings. It is used for very informal dining.

General Guidelines Dishwashers are not sterling-silver friendly. The vibrations subject the soft metal to scratches and water spots leave marks on the surface. The heat of the machine also tends to soften the metal. Handwashing is recommended. Another way to take care of sterling silver is to use it all the time. As time goes on and it is exposed to the air, a patina forms giving it a lustrous and mellow finish.

48

Flatware Design

A spoon was probably the first eating utensil and was designed from shells. Eventually spoons were carved from wood and then shaped from horns. These early utensils did not last long and very few survived to this day. As people began to work with various types of metals, they ultimately turned to fashion-eating implements and then to spoon-shaped utensils.

Spoons also began to change when forks were introduced. Large spoons became tablespoons and smaller spoons became teaspoons.

Teaspoons were developed as a necessary implement for drinking tea, which was introduced into England around the sixteen hundreds and became part of daily life in the American colonies by the seventeen hundreds. When tea was first introduced to Europe, the tea leaves were eaten; but after learning more about tea, people used teaspoons to remove the floating tea leaves and to stir sugar and cream into the tea.

Knives have been around a long time, yet few early examples exist today since continuous use and sharpening eventually wore them out. In Sheffield, England, beginning in the early twelve hundreds, the wealthy people of that time used knives made of silver or gold and some even had precious stones set into the handles. People had their own flatware and carried it on their person wherever they went because not everyone had individual implements for their guests. In fact, the inns of that time did not furnish guests with knives and spoons.

The shape of knife blades has changed from time to time for various reasons. It was reported that Cardinal Richelieu (seventeen hundreds) had a guest that habitually picked his teeth at the table with the point of his knife. This so enraged the Cardinal that he ordered all blades of knives used at the dinner table to be blunt. Another tale was that it was dangerous to use pointed knives at the table. When tempers flared, blunt knives caused less injury; therefore in 1669, King Louis IV passed a law making pointed knives illegal at the table.

Another reason for changes in the blade shape was style. Stainless steel inserts called "findings" fit into sterling handles and provided the best blades. Before stainless steel, one type of knife blade produced was made from plain steel—sometimes silver plated. These silver-plated blades reacted to too many food items and salts and became pitted or damaged. Many of these knives were thrown out. This accounts for the fact that many old sets have few knives or none at all. Another problem was stress that often caused some blades to snap. Eventually, a number of manufacturers produced blades in all kinds of styles that silversmiths inserted into sterling handles. Today knives come in a large variety of shapes with different styles and sizes in blades.

Fashion in Europe during the nineteenth century downplayed the usage of the knife to such an extent that one was not only to use it as little as possible but also to put it aside when it was not in use. One should cut up his or her food with the knife in the more capable hand and the fork in the other; one should then put down the knife, being careful to place it with the blade's edge toward the center of the plate, not facing other diners. Then the fork changed hands and was used to take the cut food to the mouth.

The fork was the last item to become a part of everyday eating utensils. The first record of one was in an inventory taken in the Italian city of Florence in 1361. Catherine de Medici, an Italian noblewoman who later became Queen of France, brought several dozen forks with her when she arrived in that country in 1533. The fork was slowly introduced into the homes of the wealthy in France and was even more slowly introduced into England. In 1611, Thomas Coryate claimed that he was the first Englishman to eat with a fork in London. He had encountered forks during his travels around the Continent. James Cross Giblin reported that by 1650 the fork was in use in almost all of England.

In the next one hundred years, between 1650 and 1750, people changed their style of eating because of the introduction of the fork. With all these changes, the need for étiquette books about dining also emerged. One of the first books to appear in print was written by a French priest who gave explicit instructions as to how to use the knife, fork, and spoon, as well as the table napkin.

Salad-fork design owes its existence to étiquette rules introduced by the French in the nineteenth century. It was considered inappropriate to cut delicate lettuce leaves with a knife since steel blades would discolor the greens and create an undesirable metallic taste. Thus, the French kept separate silver salad forks especially for eating their salad. Around the same time the English created the broad-tined salad fork. Victorian hosts and hostesses were fond of highly specific and elaborately decorated flatware and they used this fork instead of a knife for cutting tender vegetables. The salad fork was made with an extra-wide left tine that was sometimes notched or beveled to provide extra strength and a sharp point for cutting thick veins of lettuce or broad-leaf vegetables. Other forks made with wide left tines were fish forks, dessert forks, and pastry forks. These were used to cut foods that normally did not require a knife.

As the world slipped into the Age of Industrialization (late eighteenth century and early nineteenth century), changes took place with the manufacture of flatware. Items that had been luxuries soon became more affordable. Eventually, matching sets of silver were manufactured. During the 1840s the process of silver plating was perfected and basic eating utensils became readily available.

As the silver industry continued to develop, the introduction of machinery made the production of a number of items easier and consistent in form. Previously, silver had been handmade and the pieces varied ever so slightly. Shortly after the Civil War, silversmiths began the process of marking items as sterling. The items produced represented a .925% pureness of silver. Some silversmiths marked their sterling silver as ".925" or "925/1000." The move to sterling grade was truly a significant achievement.

Up until the mid-eighteen hundreds silver was only for the very wealthy. Once silver plating was invented in the 1840s the whole dynamic changed. Almost everyone suddenly could afford to buy all types of tableware. At the same time, more modern stoves came about changing the way Americans cooked and entertained. Slowly, more foods were easily acquired (the more exotic the better) due to new refrigerated railroad cars, and dining utensils were now being made for anything edible. In an eighty-year period (1840s to 1920s), utensils went from basic knives, forks, and spoons to well over one hundred different dining implements. The peak period was from the 1880s to the 1920s.

During the development of the silver industry, settlement and exploration of the American West began to expand and this resulted in finding silver in many mining operations. With the discovery of the vast silver deposits of the Comstock Silver Mine from 1859 to 1862 and again from 1873 to 1882, silver became much more available and eventually more affordable. Other mines were also producing silver. The price of silver that had hovered around $1.35 per troy ounce suddenly dropped to $.61 per troy ounce because of the volume of silver coming into the market. The silver industry expanded, and the designs of many silver patterns reflected the increased ability of manufacturers to produce pleasing designs and patterns. The increased refinement in everyday dining also added to the expansion of the industry. As silver dropped in price, causing sterling to become more affordable, the manufacturers increased their production. The expansion of silver designs of the time represented many of the current interests in art and history.

Several silver manufacturers in the United States traveled to England about this time and returned with designers and workers. All of the silver manufacturers had creative people at work in design and production. One of the truly outstanding geniuses from England was William C. Codman. He produced a number of important designs for the American firm Gorham, some of which survive to this day—almost one hundred years after their introduction. He was also very important in the development of Gorham's Martele, or hammered silver. Reed and Barton had Ernest Meyer who was responsible for Francis I which was the most popular pattern for that company.

One of the best examples of the burgeoning worldwide recognition of silver was the public's response to the display of Tiffany & Company at the Paris Exposition held in 1878. The company received numerous awards for its silver designs and especially for its display of the Mackay silver service designed by Edward Moore. The Mackay family owned part of the Comstock Mine contracted with Tiffany to produce a silver service made from Mackay's own silver deposits. Tiffany required the work of over two hundred men working for a period of two years to complete the service that consisted of approximately twelve hundred and fifty pieces of flatware and hollowware. Tiffany was perhaps the most exclusive American silver manufacturer. Its silver was heavier in weight, had distinctive designs, and was exclusive because it could be purchased only at Tiffany's owned stores.

The years between 1860 and World War I were the Golden Age of table manners, and American travelers returning from the Continent brought back a taste for specialized tableware. At the same time, the adaptation of the steam engine to manufacturing and the discovery of new silver deposits set off a boom in American tableware production. As both cuisine and étiquette became more sophisticated, unique utensils began to appear. There was the bread fork, used to hold a loaf in place while it was cut. There were ice-cream forks, corn scrapers, and implements designed specifically for baked potatoes, piccalilli, chowchow, and anchovies, among other food items. In recent years there has been a revival of interest in Victorian tableware, but some items are simply too specialized to ever regain currency. Who needs a Saratoga chip server when nobody even remembers what Saratoga chips were? Butter pick forks are of limited use when you're serving bowls of extra virgin olive oil with your bread. And please be honest—when was the last time you really needed a claret muddler or a pair of sardine spades?

Repousse silver (ruh-poo-SAY) is made by taking a sheet of silver and pressing it into a mold from the back. The molded piece is then taken out of the mold and worked from the front of the piece with various tools such as chisels to provide higher relief or definition to the design. Repousse antique pieces are prized because of their rarity and because the patina or tarnish highlights the design elements giving the silver a very three-dimensional look.

Grande Baroque is one of Wallace's most enduring and sophisticated sterling silver flatware patterns. Ornately sculpted into a three-dimensional work of art, the handle of each piece curves lavishly into flowers with the classical acanthus leaf. The table that is set with Grande Baroque is a sumptuous one indeed.

Wallace Grand Baroque Silver was designed by renowned silversmith William Warren in the year 1941.

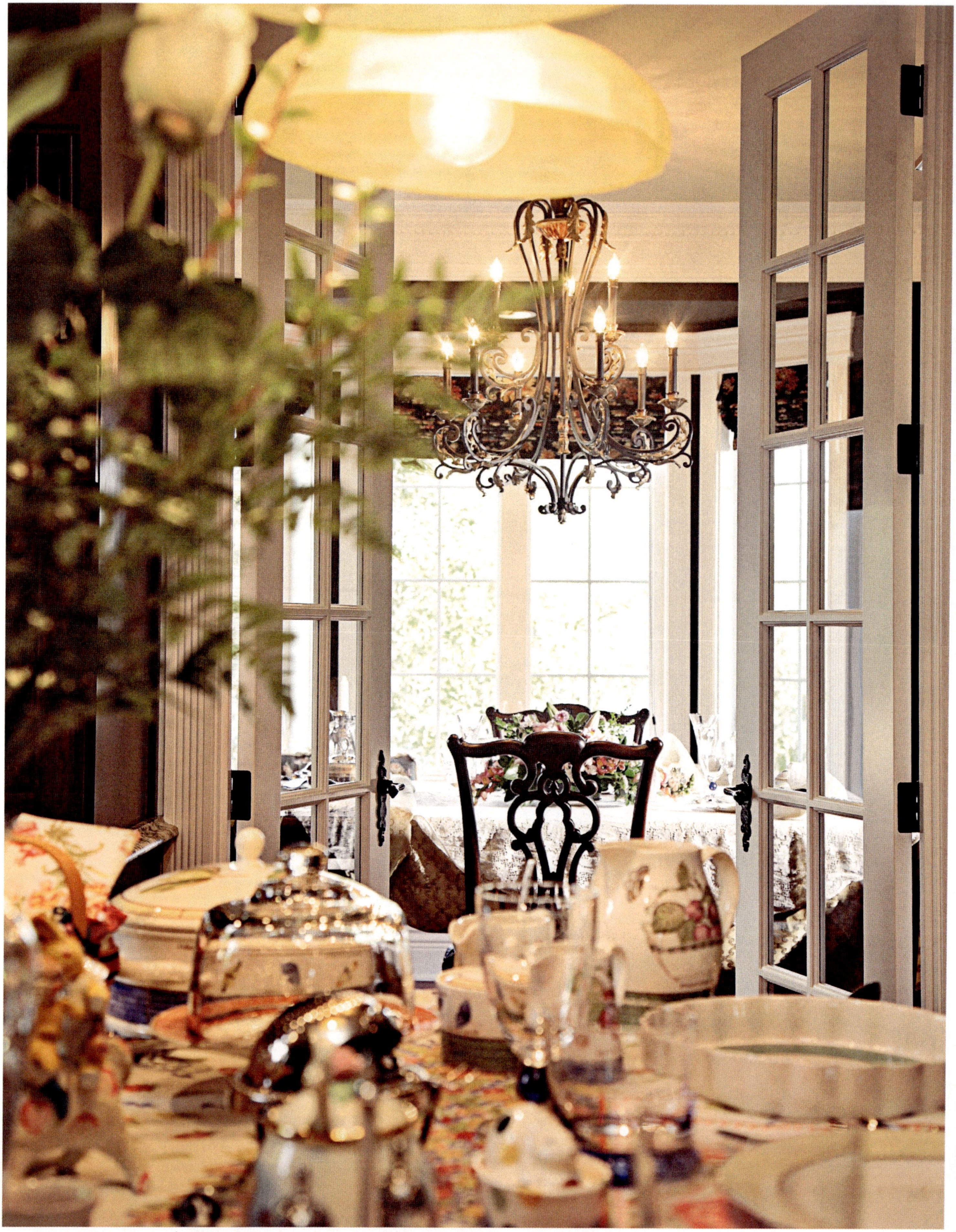

Dinnerware

It is interesting to note that the word "china" was first used in England to describe porcelain pieces simply because the first pieces to be seen came from China. As it is used today, the word should describe only porcelain dinnerware. Porcelain china is divided into three groups—soft-paste, hard-paste and bone china.

Pottery pieces should be referred to as earthenware or stone china because, although glazed, they are not made with a porcelain process. They are fired at a lower temperature than china and the ingredients, although similar, are combined in different proportions. Pottery pieces are porous while china pieces are not.

Ceramic is a term used for anything made from baked clay but is not used to refer to china.

Porcelain This is made from a combination of clays—kaolin, quartz, and feldspar. It is fired at a very high temperature to make the material extremely hard. Porcelain is nonporous, smooth, and translucent because the high firing has made it vitrified. It is literally glass like. If you hold a porcelain plate to the light and pass your hand behind it, you will see its shadow. Some of the most famous makers of porcelain include Rosenthal, Lenox, Noritake, and, of course, all the French manufacturers from the town of Limoges, France. Some people believe porcelain teapots make the best tea. Porcelain should never be placed in the dishwasher.

Bone China This is a type of porcelain that contains bone ash (usually ox bone) or a chemical equivalent to whiten it. There is no difference in quality between porcelain and bone china. The distinction is in the color of the material. Bone china is a creamy white; porcelain has a more grayish cast. Both are considered fine china. English potters invented bone china and English manufacturers are in the forefront of producers today. Wedgwood, Royal Crown Derby, Royal Doulton, Minton, and Spode are just a few of the famous brands. Bone china should never be placed in the dishwasher.

Earthenware Made from heavier, less refined clays, earthenware is fired at much lower temperatures making it possible to produce very strong, bright colors—Fiestaware is a good example. Earthenware is slightly porous and is not as strong as fine china; it is opaque. The shadow of your hand will not be visible if you hold it up to the light. Earthenware may be placed in the dishwasher.

Stoneware The link between earthenware and china, stoneware is usually semi-vitrified. In appearance, it seems very much like earthenware with its heavier weight and earthy colored body. In strength and durability, however, it is much closer to china. Neither earthenware nor stoneware is used at a formal dinner. Some of the best-known stoneware comes from the Arabia factory in Finland. Stoneware may be placed in the dishwasher.

Dinnerware History

Perhaps the most important contribution China made to European life, second only to tea, was "china" itself—the hard-translucent glazed pottery the Chinese invented during the Tang dynasty which we also know as porcelain. China had long since exported porcelain over the Silk Route to Persia and Turkey and fine examples of pre-fifteenth century china are still in everyday use. In Europe before the dawn of the China trade, the highest achievement of the potter's art was a kind of earthenware, which was fired, then coated with an opaque glaze and fired again, fixing the colors with which it had been painted. This method was generally named for its supposed place of origin and was known as majolica in Italy, faience in France, Delft in the Low Countries, and so forth. The Netherlands tin-glazed Dutch earthenware was beautifully designed with blue and white or polychrome decorations. No earthenware could stand up to boiling water without dissolving and nowhere in Europe was it understood how to heat a kiln to the fourteen hundred degrees or so required to vitrify clay and make it impervious to liquids—boiling or not. Even so wise a man as Sir Francis Bacon could only view porcelain as a kind of plaster, which after a long lapse of time buried in the earth, "congealed and glazed itself into that fine substance." Other writers speculated it was made from lobster shell or eggs pounded into dust.

Porcelain, in time, became the only Chinese import to rival tea in popularity. The wealthy collected it on a grand scale. An English diplomat once collected almost five tons of Ming pieces while serving in Iran in 1875. Even middle-class people became so carried away that Daniel Defoe could complain of china "on every chimney piece, to the tops of ceilings, until it became a grievance." Such abundance half the world away from its place of manufacture was due in part to its use as ships' ballast. The China trade came to rest on two water-sensitive, high-value commodities—silk and tea. These had to be carried in the middle of the ship to prevent water damage; but to trim the ship and make her sail properly, about half the cargo's weight (not volume) was needed below the waterline in the bilges. Very roughly, a quarter of all tea imported had to be matched by ballast; and from the ships' records available, it appears that about a quarter of all ballast was porcelain. Over the course of the seventeen hundreds, England probably imported twenty-four thousand tons of porcelain while a roughly equal amount would have been imported into Europe and the American colonies.

To keep up with this demand, Jingdezhen, China's main porcelain-making center since the Song dynasty, as early as 1712, needed to keep three thousand kilns fired day and night. The prices fell to ridiculously low levels—seven pounds seven shillings in 1730 for a tea service for two hundred people—each piece ornamented with the crest of the ambassador who placed the order. Five thousand teapots were ordered in 1732 for two pence each. Even if we multiply these prices by one hundred to approximate the current rates, it is an incredibly cheap price for porcelain of this quality. Before European-made wares came into general use around the eighteen hundreds, the English and European middle classes enjoyed their tea and meals from the finest quality chinaware.

For years before the advent of tea, it had been the dream of all European potters to produce china themselves. Britains Elers' brothers mastered stoneware, but their efforts to reproduce china proved unavailing, and so did the efforts of all the other first-rate potters in Europe. The potters of St. Cloud in France developed a substitute now known as soft-paste porcelain, but nobody came near approximating the real thing until an apothecary's apprentice named Johann Friedrich Böttger bumbled onto the scene.

When he was nineteen, Böttger met a mysterious alchemist, Lascaris, in Berlin and received a gift of transmutation powder from him. It was a belief at the time that a skilled alchemist, such as Lascaris, could use the secrets of transmutation with a secret powder to change, or transmute, certain basic metals into gold. As Lascaris no doubt intended, Böttger couldn't resist publicizing the powder's powers. Unfortunately, he also claimed to have made it himself with the predictable result that he soon had all the crowned heads of Germany after him to produce the expected transmutation of metal into gold. He sought safety in Dresden under the protection of Augustus II, "the Strong," Elector of Saxony and King of Poland. But with extravagant and riotous living, his stock of powder was soon exhausted and his "protector" proved not to be the disinterested well-wisher he seemed. Poor Böttger found himself confined in the castle of Konigstein where he was given a laboratory for his research and a clear understanding of the fate reserved for him should he fail in transmutation. He finally convinced his jailer, a certain Count Tschirnhaus, that he was not adept in the transmutation arts but merely a demonstrator. The Count proposed that he should put the laboratory to use in the secret quest of making china, since next to gold and power, collecting Japanese and Chinese porcelains was Augustus' ruling passion. He had filled a palace with his collection of some twenty thousand pieces—which was still growing by the time of his death. Fortunately for Böttger, Saxony was blessed with the two main ingredients for the manufacture of porcelain-china clay or kaolin and the so-called china stone—a type of rock made up mostly of silica and alumina that serves as a flux and gives the ware its translucency. Böttger first produced stoneware and then, after numerous false starts, finally obtained hard-paste red porcelain in 1703. The kiln was kept burning for five days and five nights and, in anticipation of success, his royal patron had been invited to see it opened. It is reported that the first product Böttger took out and presented to Augustus was a fine red teapot. The long-sought secret had been discovered at last and after a few more years Böttger managed to come up with genuine hard-paste white porcelain.

Completely restored to favor, Böttger admitted he had never possessed the secret of transmutation. He was formally forgiven and in 1710 was promptly appointed director of Europe's first china factory (Royal Saxon Porcelain Manufactory). The factory was established near Dresden in a little village called Meissen and proved to be a bonanza for Augustus. Soon after full production got underway in 1713, the export market for Meissen figurines alone ran into the millions. In a letter in 1746, Horace Walpole grumbled about the new fashion in table decoration at the banquets of the English nobility—"Jellies, biscuits, sugar, plums, and cream have long since given way to harlequins, gondoliers, Turks, Chinese, and shepherdesses of Saxon China." Teapots and teacups were also produced in ever increasing quantities.

Industrial espionage spread the secret of porcelain manufacturing beyond the German borders during the 1740s. In 1751, fifteen English entrepreneurs joined together to create the Worchester Royal Porcelain Works. In France, to the chagrin of every prince and duke lavishing patronage on their own little porcelain works, King Louis XV's beloved Madame De Pompadour decided to bestow her patronage on a little factory located near Versailles at Sevres. To please her, the King bought it in 1759 and, just to make sure it would prosper, ordered the royal chinaware be made there. When in need of money the King sometimes forced the courtiers at Versailles to buy quantities of porcelain from Sevres at exorbitant prices.

In 1760 Josiah Wedgwood produced the first commercially successful earthenware that was pale enough to resemble porcelain. It was named creamware and has been called Britain's great contribution in the history of ceramics. It could be painted or printed like porcelain—usually after glazing. Queen Charlotte was so pleased with the ware she allowed it to be called Queensware.

Perhaps the most famous dinner service in the world was the 952-piece creamware set produced by Wedgwood for Empress Catherine of Russia around 1774. It was decorated with 1,244 scenic views of Great Britain.

The English porcelain firms of the eighteenth century kept experimenting with the formulae filched from the Continent and it would be interesting indeed to know how J. Spode first hit upon the idea of using the ingredient that distinguishes English from all other porcelains—the ashes of burned bones. Bone ash is combined with china clay—thus giving it more stability. From the beginning, tea equipage was the mainstay of the production at Worchester, Chelsea, Spode, Limoges, and all the other centers of china manufacturing in Europe.

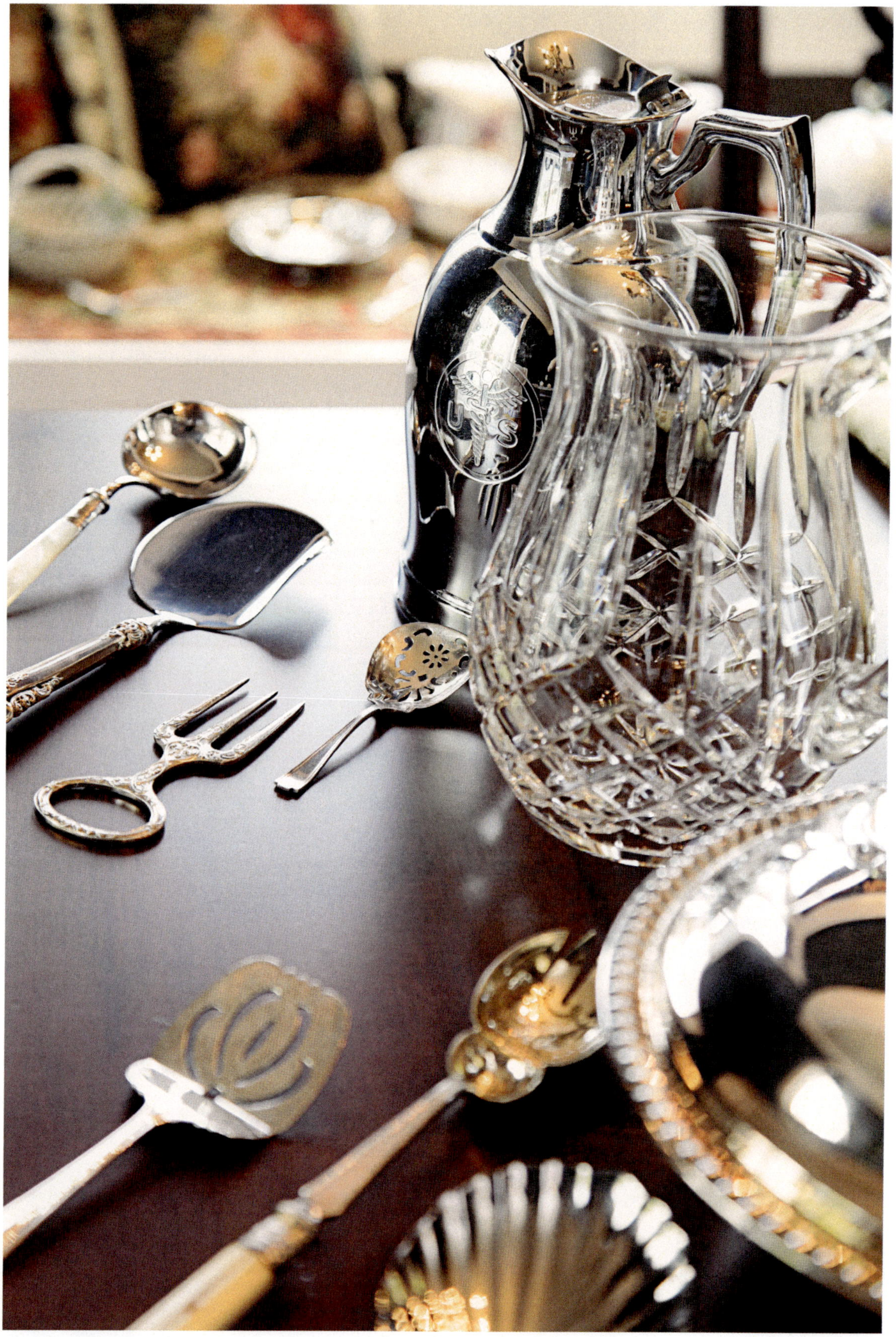

Crystal

Crystal adds to sensory pleasure at the table. Visually, it catches the light; to the touch and taste, it adds enjoyment. During the middle ages, the method of producing crystal, fine stemware, and vessels was only known to a few—the few being the glassmakers of Murano, Italy. They were elevated to the level of nobility. By the early twentieth century, however, lead crystal was an easily acquired luxury.

Most people call fine stemware crystal. But the word "crystal" simply means clear, uncolored stemware. When people refer to crystal, they mean lead crystal. A glass must be made of at least twenty-four percent lead to carry this appellation legally. Lead gives stemware more weight, increases its resilience, and adds brilliance and sparkle. It is most often used to make stemware with cut patterns because it provides a thicker wall with which the cutter can work. It will also reflect a virtual rainbow of lights when polished.

62

Stemware

Stemware is a general term used to refer to drinkware that has some type of stem. Stem styles vary in length and girth. There are many variations and designs of stemware. Each style is unique and serves a multitude of purposes.

Goblet This is the largest piece of stemware; it holds from nine to twelve fluid ounces. It is always used for water in formal dining, but at an informal dinner, its use is optional.

Red Wine Today, with the exception of Waterford, most formal patterns offer just one size of red wine glasses. Burgundy and Bordeaux have their own special stemware. An all-purpose wine glass will have a rounded bowl that tapers slightly toward the rim to contain the wine's bouquet.

White Wine A white wine glass has a bowl that is smaller than red, and the sides are a little straighter because white wine does not have as intense an aroma as red. Never fill more than half of a stemware in order to concentrate on the wine's more delicate bouquet.

Hock Wine These are white wines from the Rhine Valley and are named for their growing area, Hockenheim. Initially, Hock wines were served in stemware with a colored bowl to hide the wine's cloudiness, but today these wines are no longer cloudy. Queen Victoria, whose ancestors on her mother's side were from the house of Saxony Cobert, introduced Hock wines to England. Rhine wines are served in long-stemmed glasses with small squared-off bowls. These are often not available as part of a regular stemware pattern.

Champagne The most common shape available today is the flute which has a long, narrow bowl to preserve the effervescence of the bubbles. It has supplanted the traditional saucer champagne, which has a shallow wide bowl, letting bubbles escape too quickly to today's tastes. In the past, a gentleman always carried his own swizzle stick which he used to take out the bubbles—not make more.

Cocktail Strictly speaking, a cocktail glass should not be included in a formal stemware grouping; cocktails are never served at the formal dining table.

Cordial There are many different after-dinner drinks, and almost every single one has its own special glass. Cordial glasses are never flared because the cordial's aroma must be contained in the glass so the drinker can savor it. These glasses have very small bowls because liqueurs are very concentrated and only a small amount is taken.

Sherry The one apéritif that is still used at a formal table is the sherry glass to accompany the soup course. Today, it is rarely available in stemware patterns but is sold as a specialty glass.

Dining Out

Once a person steps out of his or her home to enjoy a meal, knowing how to dine properly is of great value. How to enter a room, how to enter a restaurant, or how to leave a dinner party early becomes useful information in certain situations. The following chapter explains in great detail all the aspects of enjoying a meal away from home.

Fashionably on Time Arrive at a formal dinner party or a formal event thirty minutes before the scheduled time of the affair. At a less formal dinner or less formal event, the general rule today is to arrive no earlier than twenty minutes. Gifts are not expected unless it is a birthday or a celebration of some sort. You may bring a special bottle of vintage port, champagne, or sparkling cider. Never suggest or mention that your wine be served. The host or hostess has decided which wines should accompany his or her menu.

Flowers should not be given to the hostess because she or the staff will be too preoccupied to arrange them. The flowers, like the wine, have already been chosen. Instead, it is thoughtful to call the hostess several days before the event to say you would like to send her flowers in advance and ask what her favorite flowers are as well as her preference in color.

Hostess gifts began in the USA in the 1930s and reached Britain in the 1950s. During that time, it was customary to bring chocolates. Today it is still customary to bring chocolates, but a bottle of Champagne is always greatly appreciated.

Making an Entrance Almost everyone watches the entrance of a room. Enter the room with good posture. Do not rush into the room even if you are late. Do not speak loudly or expect everyone to stop what they are doing and greet you. Rather, look for the honoree, the host, or the hostess and greet them politely while complimenting the hostess on some item of décor, her outfit, etc. It is true you only get one chance to make a first impression; be careful your impression is a good one. Always be sure to greet the host or hostess before you accept a drink.

People evaluate you within three to seven seconds when you first meet them. Say something positive. Do not say, "Sorry to interrupt," because it is negative. Say, "May I join you?" or say, "How do you do?" Ask questions to promote conversation such as: "How do you spend most of your time?" or, "How was your journey today?"

Avoid sex, money, politics, and religion as initial subject matter.

Removing Gloves Remove your gloves before you shake a person's hand. Unless there is a reason not to, it is best to remove your gloves as soon as you arrive at an event.

Gloves are often thought of as something born of the Napoleonic era. In fact, they've been worn for over 10,000 years. Of course, the earliest uses were not for fashion but for more utilitarian in purpose. Gloves protected one's hands from harsh weather or hard labor. Even thousands of years ago, they were not worn during dinner service. This is understandable when you consider that until the sixteen hundreds food was traditionally eaten with fingers.

Taking Your Seat at the Table Men and women are expected to enter and sit in a chair from their left sides. This prevents bumping their neighbors when seating. The exception is when the chairs are too close to enter from the side and must be pulled out to sit. Exit the chair the same way you entered. Do not forget to push the chair back in when you leave. A gentleman should seat a lady by standing behind her chair and pulling it back with both hands. When she is half seated, the chair should gently be pushed forward so her chair is under her hips. After seating her, the gentleman takes the seat to her left. Good posture is important; do not slouch.

Men are seated to the left of the woman so as to have their right hand available to assist the woman.

Push sweater or sleeves up above elbow before eating.

Rest your wrists on the table, not your elbows.

Knowing Your Space at the Table Your space should be confined to the imaginary box around you. If you must move your feet, do so in your own foot space (close to the floor and within the chair legs). If you are not eating, your hands should be on your lap or on the table right in front of you. While you are eating, try to put your non-eating hand on your lap. If you must rest your hands on the table, do so with your wrists only. As mentioned above, place your wrists in front of you on the edge of the table. Do not put your elbows on the table.

Placing Purses, Briefcases, Eyeglasses, and Eyeglass Cases Do not place any items on the table. A small purse should go on your lap under the napkin. A large purse, briefcase, and other personal items should go under your chair, out of the way. Never block the path of other guests or the serving staff. An eyeglass case belongs in your purse or pocket. Never put your eyeglasses on the table. Your cell phone should be set to vibrate or switched off and put away. It is extremely rude to make or accept a phone call (or text) during a meal.

Lavatory: Women go to the "powder room" and men go to "freshen up."

Proper Way to Leave an Event or Someone's Home The general rule for leaving an event is approximately forty-five minutes after the meal is over.

Hosting an Event at a Restaurant Entertain at a restaurant with which you are familiar. If you never have eaten at a particular restaurant, check it out well in advance. Be sure the maître d' knows who you are, how many guests you are expecting, and where you want to be seated. This is especially important for a business discussion when a quiet area is needed.

Choose a table that is well away from the kitchen, lavatories, and cocktail area. These are high traffic areas and not conducive to privacy. If there are only two of you, do not sit directly across from your guest. Seat your guest to your right, if possible. When hosting two guests at a table, which accommodates four, seat the senior person on your right and the other person across from you, leaving the seat to your left empty. It is your job to indicate where you wish your guests to sit and they should be seated before you sit.

Seat your guests in the best seats. Do not seat them with their backs to the room or to a window if there is a view. Also, if there are unmatched chairs, be sure your guests have the most comfortable seats.

On the day of the event, reconfirm the time and place with your guests or their representative(s). Arrive early to check on the seating arrangements and arrange for payment with the maître d'. Guests should never be confronted accidentally with a check nor should you pay in front of them. This calls attention to financial details which will only detract from the event. It also prevents guests from trying to pay the check. If guests want to pay, assure them it has "already been taken care of." This is especially handy when a woman hosts an event.

Restaurant Vocabulary

À la carte – The main course comes by itself, without side dishes, salad, etc.

À la mode – In America this usually applies to ice cream being placed with dessert; it may also refer to beef with vegetables in sauce.

Alfresco – This means to eat outdoors, often on a patio.

Bon appétit – While the literal translation is good appetite, it means have a good meal.

Maître d' – The head waiter in a restaurant.

Soupe du jour – The translation is soup of the day and usually means it is in addition to the other soups on the menu.

Table d'hôtes – A complete meal—the opposite of à la carte.

The Étiquette of Tipping Good service should be rewarded. The amount of the tip varies from the type of situation, location, etc. It also varies from country to country. Because many countries in Europe pay their staff as if they were engaged in a profession, rather than working at a job, they do not expect large tips. In some countries, tipping is not expected at all. When traveling, research the tipping customs of unfamiliar countries before you leave home. The following rules are for American establishments:

Restaurant Tip 15% to 20% of the bill. If you are part of a large party, be sure to check whether the gratuity already has been added to the check. This often is done in many restaurants.

Country Club Personnel Depending on the level of service and the club's tipping policy, $5 - $20 for errands such as sending a fax, making dinner or other reservations, or securing opera or theatre tickets. A larger gratuity at Christmas for special or favored service providers is also appropriate.

Coat Check or Ladies' Room Attendants A $1 - $2 tip each is customary.

Cab or Car Service Driver Tip 15% of the fare.

Concierge Tip $10 - $15 for more difficult or timely tasks.

Maid Service at Hotel or Bed and Breakfast Tip $5 a day for each day of your stay. Consider padding the tip a bit for especially attentive staff.

Spa Staff Tip 15% - 20% of the total bill evenly and divide among treatment specialists.

The custom of tipping finds its roots in tea—more specifically, the colorful tea gardens of eighteenth-century England. As these "pleasure gardens" grew more popular and elaborate, venues such as Vauxhall Gardens in London became the most fashionable public entertainment of the day luring musicians, magicians, comedians, and actors to perform for the crowds and offering such extravagant diversions as hot-air balloon rides and fireworks displays. For guests, the sharing of tea was the highlight of the evening. To help compensate servers, locked wooden boxes were placed on tables throughout the gardens at seating areas, each inscribed with the letters T.I.P.S.—"To Insure Prompt Service." It became convention to drop coins into the box as an added enticement to servers, and the custom has endured.

Graceful Dining Manners

Manners and good behavior suddenly are revealed during a meal. Good table manners are one of the most visible signs of proper étiquette. This chapter will cover many styles of dining and will enhance any individual's knowledge of dining successfully.

Continental (European) and American Dining with a Knife and Fork

Continental Style Dining Continental dining dictates utensils may be held in your hands throughout the meal. The knife is held in your right hand and the fork in your left hand with tines facing down. Hold the utensils in a relaxed manner using your forefingers as guides.

Cut the food one or two pieces at a time. Secure the food with the fork and convey it to your mouth. You may push food onto the backside of the fork with the knife. Even though Continental dining dictates you should keep the utensils in your hands at all times, you may need to rest them if you take a drink or retire momentarily to the lavatory. If you decide to rest the utensils, place them in resting positions using a clock as a guide. The knife resting position is 12 o'clock and 3 o'clock on the plate with the sharp side of the blade facing you. The fork resting position is 7 o'clock on the plate with tines facing down. When you are finished eating, place the knife with the sharp side of the blade facing you and place the fork with tines facing down to the left of the knife. Both knife and fork finish positions are 11 o'clock and 5 o'clock on the plate.

When eating, the fork with the impaled food enters the mouth with the tines facing down. Remember, the impaled food must be balanced on the back of the fork tines. As it is extremely difficult to eat like this; it is considered the height of good manners!

Continental Style Resting Positions for Knife and Fork

Tines Facing Down

Continental Style Finish Positions for Knife and Fork

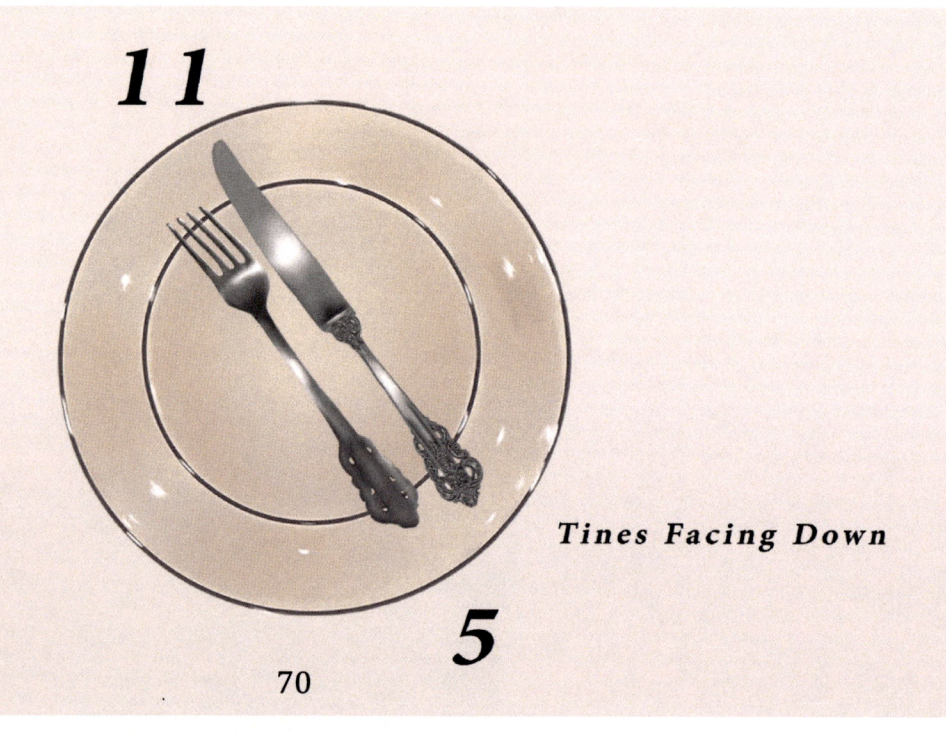

Tines Facing Down

American Style Dining American dining begins in the same manner as Continental. Cut the food with the knife in your right hand and the fork in your left hand as you would in the Continental style. However, after cutting the food, place the knife with the sharp side of the blade facing you in its resting position at 12 o'clock and 3 o'clock on the plate and transfer the fork from your left hand to your right hand with tines facing up. If you wish to rest the fork, rest it in the 5 o'clock position on the plate with tines facing up. When you are finished eating, place the knife with the sharp side of the blade facing you and place the fork with tines facing up to the left of the knife. Both knife and fork finish positions are 11 o'clock and 5 o'clock on the plate.

"Right" means "correct" or "okay" in English. "Sinister" originally meant "left." In French, a just man is droit, meaning both "right" and "straight" while gauche ("left") describes one who lacks social assurance as well as dexterity. We raise our right hands to take oaths and extend them to shake hands.

Bone china and porcelain are ageless. The stark simplicity is classic and food looks beautiful against a cream background.

American Style Resting Positions for Knife and Fork

12

9   3

Tines Facing Up

6

American Style Finish Positions for Knife and Fork

11

Tines Facing Up

5

Dessert Style Dining with a Dessert Spoon and Dessert Fork Dessert should be served with a dessert spoon and dessert fork. Hold the dessert spoon in your right hand and hold the dessert fork in your left hand with tines facing down. In mimicking Continental style dining, the dessert spoon is used to cut the dessert, while the dessert fork is used to convey the dessert to one's mouth. In the English style of dining, the dessert fork serves to push the dessert onto the dessert spoon. The dessert spoon conveys the dessert to one's mouth.

For above styles of dining, the dessert spoon rest position is 5 o'clock on the plate with spoon bowl facing down and the dessert fork rest position is 7 o'clock on the plate with tines facing down. Finish positions for both the dessert spoon and dessert fork are 11 o'clock and 5 o'clock on the plate with dessert spoon bowl and dessert fork facing down.

When served dessert with <u>one</u> utensil such as a dessert spoon, the dessert spoon is held in your right hand. When served dessert with a dessert fork, the dessert fork is held in your right hand with tines facing up. Some examples of utensils held in your right hand are citrus spoons, pie forks, and ice cream forks. Rest positions for the various dessert forks are 5 o'clock on the plate with tines facing up. Rest positions for the various dessert spoons are 5 o'clock on the plate with the spoon bowls facing up. Finish positions for all utensils are 11 o'clock and 5 o'clock on the plate with fork tines and spoon bowl facing down.

If dessert is served in a stemmed glass on a service plate, the dessert spoon is placed on the service plate, never left in the glass, even when resting the dessert spoon.

If dessert is in a dish that resembles a soup plate or sauce dish, leave the dessert spoon in the bowl for rest position and on the service plate for finish position. If there is no service plate, leave it in the bowl.

Dining with Cups and Saucers When sipping tea, coffee, or other liquids from a cup, lift the cup and take a gentle sip without making any noise. The handled cup is held with your index finger through the handle, your thumb just above it to support your grip, and your second finger below the handle for added security. Your little finger should follow the curve of your other fingers and not be elevated in an affected manner. If the cup and saucer are more than twelve inches away from you, lift the cup and saucer together to take a sip. Be careful not to drop the teaspoon off the saucer. You may place the cup and saucer back on the table in between sips. Both rest and finish positions for the teaspoon are 5 o'clock on the saucer with spoon bowl facing up. The cup handle is also placed in the 5 o'clock position.

Rest and Finish Positions for Cup and Teaspoon

Dining with Stemware Hold the stemware with your thumb and first two fingers by the stem, not by the bowl. By holding the stemware in this manner, you are able to secure it and also prevent your body heat from affecting the food. Scoop the food items with the teaspoon from side to side moving from the right to the left side of the bowl of the stemware. Scoop the food items in small amounts. Put the teaspoon down each time you take a spoonful or you may hold it for short periods of time. Both rest and finish positions for the teaspoon are 5 o'clock on the plate with the spoon bowl facing up. If there is no plate, leave the teaspoon in the stemware when finished. Be careful not to knock it over.

Rest and Finish Positions for Teaspoon

Dining with Rimmed Soup Plates With the soup spoon, scoop the soup away from you and sip the soup from the side of the soup spoon rather than inserting the spoon into your mouth. If the level of the soup is so low that you must tip the rimmed soup plate, tip the rimmed soup plate away from you. Again, scoop the soup away from you.

Soup bowls should be called "rimmed soup plates."

If the soup is very chunky, scoop away and insert the soup spoon into your mouth tip first. Other examples in which you would scoop away and insert the spoon tip first are cereal, gruel, or oatmeal.

If you are served soup or bouillon from a bowl with handles and there are mushrooms, noodles, or other food items, you should eat these items first with the soup spoon. You then may pick up the bowl by the handles and drink from it. After you drink the liquid, you may scoop any remaining mushrooms, noodles, or other food items with the soup spoon again.

The rest position for the soup spoon is in the rimmed soup plate at 5 o'clock with the spoon bowl facing up. The finish position for the soup spoon is 5 o'clock on the plate with spoon bowl facing up. If there is no plate underneath the rimmed soup plate, leave the spoon in the rimmed soup plate at 5 o'clock.

Rest Position for Soup Spoon

Finish Position for Soup Spoon

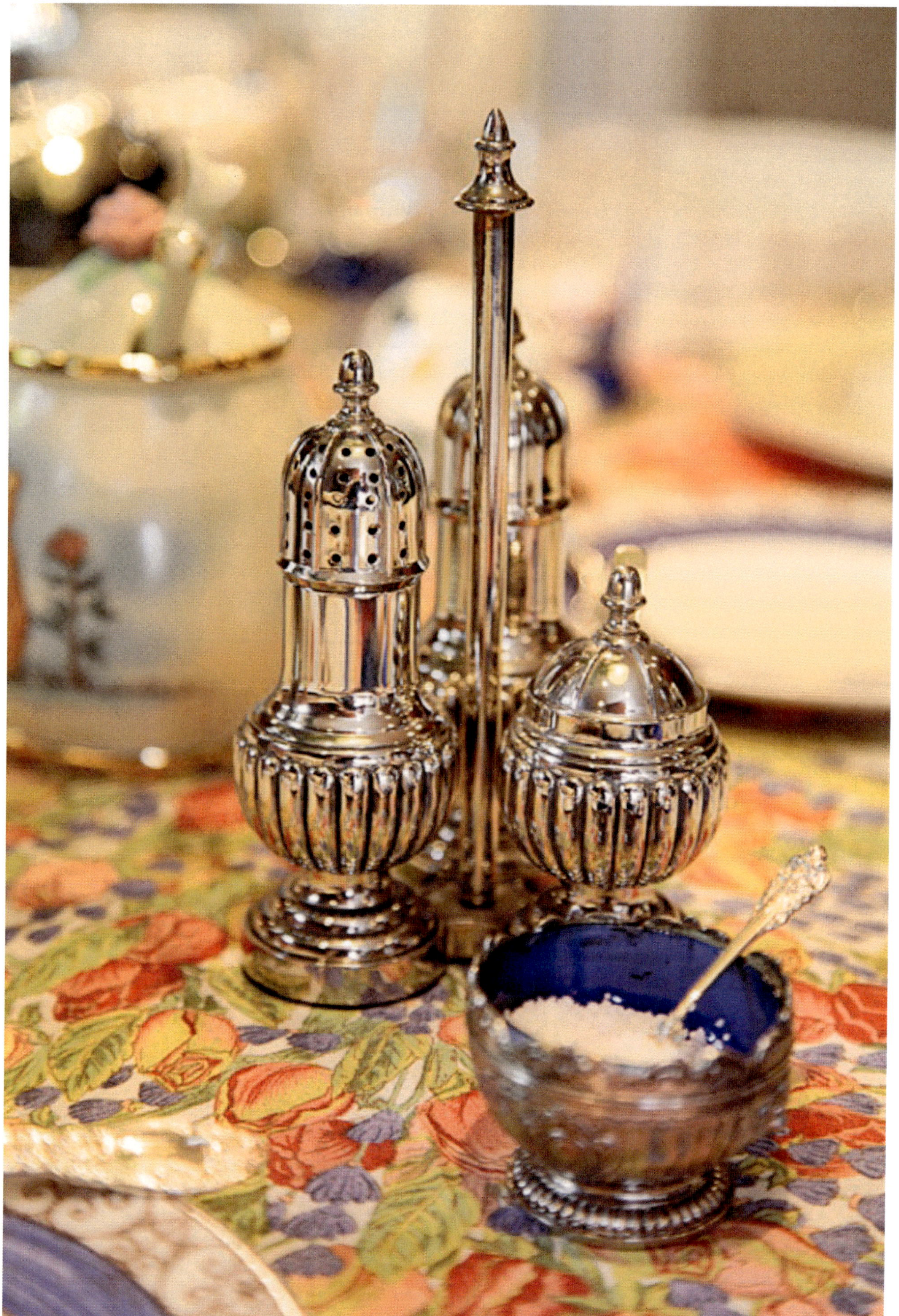

Dining at a Buffet The first thing to do at a buffet is to obtain a dinner plate. Hold the plate over your left arm on the inside of your wrist and cup the plate with your hand. When selecting food, be aware some foods will have serving utensils and some will not. If serving utensils are provided, place the food on the plate with the serving utensil. Never use a chip or any type of appetizer to serve yourself the sauce or the dip.

"Finger foods" are served at some buffets. Finger foods are categorized as foods to be eaten with one's left-hand fingers. The left hand is used for finger foods in order to keep the right hand clean to shake hands with people or to hold stemware, glasses, or cups. Some common finger food items are crackers with cheese, olives, grapes, stuffed mushrooms, breadsticks, tea sandwiches, cookies, and appetizers or hors d'œurves. If the food item is bite-size, place the whole food item in your mouth. If the food item is slightly larger, take small bites and place the remainder back on the plate. Never lick your fingers.

Étiquette dictates you must taste at least one bite of all foods served to you. To do otherwise would be rude, particularly if you are a guest at someone else's table. Do not insult your host further by saying you don't like something or by drawing attention to the situation. Keep an open mind and try bites of all foods you are served. Unless the food item is against your religion or gives you an allergic reaction, try it.

Dining with Napkins When dining, be aware when the hostess picks up her napkin and places it on her lap; you should follow suit. If there is no hostess, follow the host. Do not blot your lipstick with a cloth napkin. You should carry tissues in your purse and blot your lipstick before you begin the meal or before using the napkin.

The napkin is placed on your lap at the beginning of the meal and stays there until the meal is finished. If you must get up during the meal, place your napkin on your chair, not on the table. A used or soiled napkin should not be placed on the table until the meal is over. You will know when the meal is finished because the hostess will place her napkin on the table. She most likely will wait until everyone has finished eating before doing so. Place your used napkin to the left of the charger or dinner plate.

Napkin Dimensions

Dinner – 22-26"

Luncheon – 18-20"

Tea – 12"

Cocktail – 6-9"

The word napkin derives from the old French naperon meaning "little tablecloth." The first napkins were the size of today's bath towels. This size was practical because one ate the multicourse meal entirely with one's fingers. The ancient Egyptians, Greeks, and Romans used them to cleanse their hands during a meal, which could last many hours. At many such meals, it was proper to provide a fresh napkin with each course to keep diners from offending each other, since it was believed they would get sick watching each other wipe their mouths on filthy napkins. During the sixth century BC, Roman nobility created what we now call a "doggie bag." Guests attending a banquet were expected to wrap delicacies from the table in clean napkins to take home. It was rude to depart empty handed.

The napkin ring was introduced by the Victorian middle class to show whose napkin was whose as they would actually reuse their napkins for several consecutive meals (due to fewer staff and less money), and so patterns and designs varied to quasi-territorially mark each person's linen. Now you can buy rings of uniform design for purely decorative purposes.

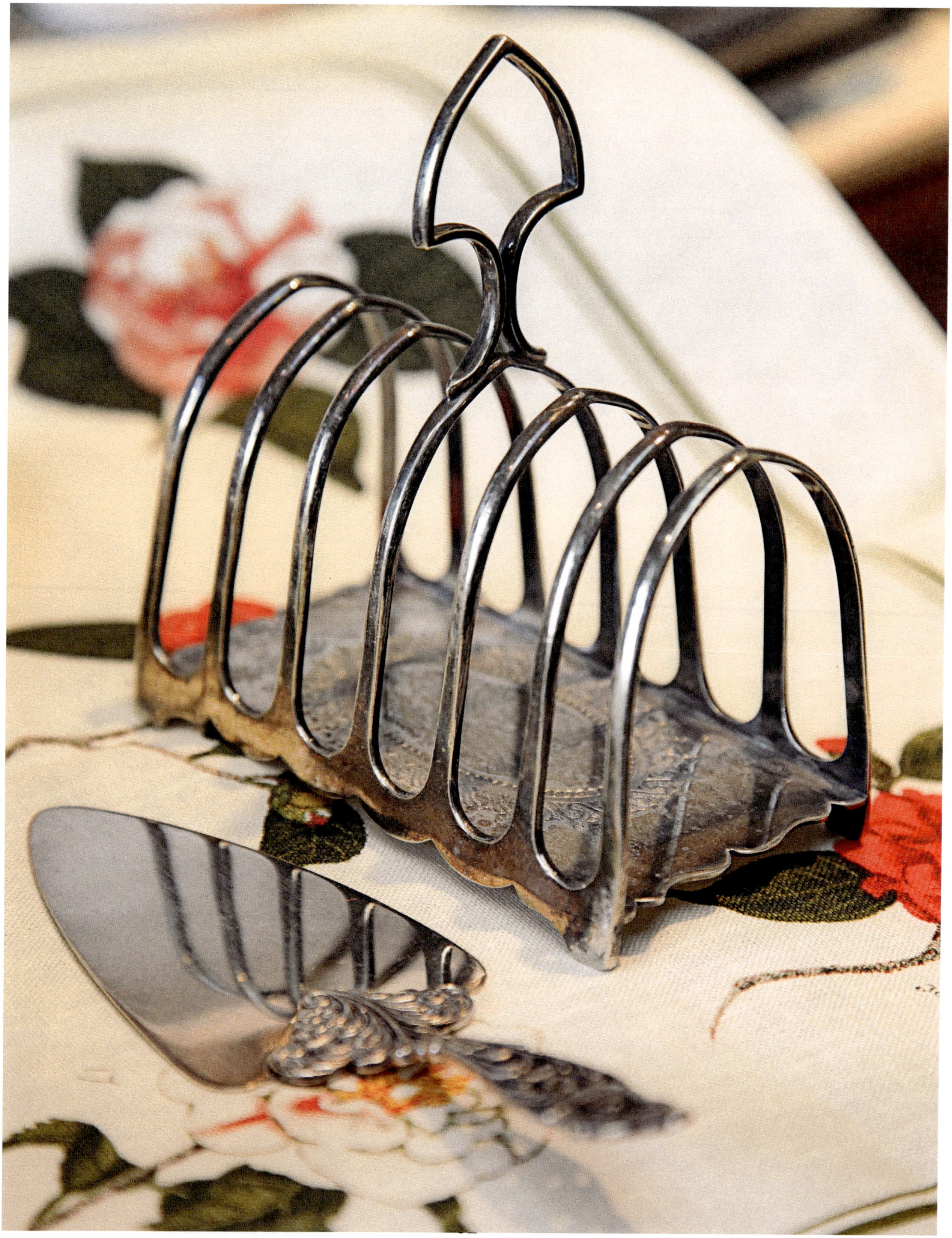

Dining with Difficult Foods

One of the most essential aspects of good table manners is to know how to eat troublesome foods. The following food items are some of the most problematic:

Artichokes Remove the leaves from the outside, working inward. Take each leaf and, if desired, dip it in the accompanying sauce or melted butter. Put it between your teeth, soft side downward, and drag it out scraping the soft side against your bottom teeth. A stuffed artichoke is eaten by spreading the stuffing with a knife on each leaf. Cut out the "choke" (the hairy center above the heart). The heart is eaten with a fork.

Avocados When the avocado is served whole or halved, within its skin, lightly hold the shell with your non-utensil hand to steady it and scoop out the pulp with the spoon. If it is served stuffed, use a fork rather than a spoon.

Cherry Tomatoes If served as an appetizer or cocktail snack, eat tomatoes with your fingers. If they are small enough to gracefully fit in your mouth whole, eat them whole because they tend to squirt when the skin is pierced. As with any other food, be careful to chew with your mouth closed. If tomatoes are part of a salad or other course, eat them with a knife and fork.

Corn on the Cob For obvious reasons, corn on the cob should never be served at a formal dinner. It is messy and lodges between one's teeth. Fresh corn can be served if it is cut from the cob before serving. In an informal situation, if corn is served on the cob, butter only each section you intend to eat as you go—minimizing the mess on hands, face, and clothing.

Cupcakes A cupcake wrapper should be removed first and placed open on the plate. After each bite, place the cupcake back on the wrapper. The rule of thumb is to do whatever is least messy and try not to attract attention.

Dessert Crêpes Dessert crêpes may be eaten with a dessert spoon and dessert fork or simply with a dessert fork.

Lemon Wedges To reduce the risk of the lemon juice squirting someone, put a fork (preferably a lemon or cocktail fork if present) into the wedge before squeezing it.

Mussels, Oysters, and Clams These foods are often served in shells or on half shells with or without broth. Each mussel, oyster, or clam shell is held in your left hand and speared with a small oyster fork held in your right hand. Lift the mussel, oyster, or clam whole from the shell and detach it. Dip it into the cocktail sauce container on your own plate. A separate bowl or plate is usually provided for the empty shells. To eat the remaining broth, you may use a spoon or you may tear up pieces of bread, spear them with a fork, and dip them in the broth before eating.

Olives Olives served as hors d'œuvres, if stuffed, are popped into your mouth with your fingers. In an informal setting where you are served whole olives with pits, eat each olive with your fingers. Remove the pit from your mouth with your cupped hand and transfer the pit on the plate.

Pasta Most pasta should be eaten with a fork. The exception is thick pasta, such as lasagna, which is easier to eat after cutting with a knife and fork. In America, pasta (spaghetti, linguini, and fettuccini) is twirled around a fork using a large spoon against the fork. The preferred "Italian" method never uses a spoon, only a fork. One would be looked down upon in Italy if caught using a spoon. Pasta should also be served in a pasta plate not a bowl.

Potatoes Whole potatoes or yams are usually cut in half with a knife then split open with your fingers. If you are adding butter, sour cream, salt, or pepper, mix it in with the fork. If you wish to eat the potato skin, cut it with a knife and fork—one or two pieces at a time. On the rare occasion that French fried potatoes are served at a formal meal, eat them with a fork.

Salad Cut large pieces of lettuce with a fork. If this is too difficult, you may use a knife and fork.

Shrimp Cocktail If the shrimp are not jumbo size or prawns, they probably can be eaten in one bite. If they are beyond bite-size, steady the plate or bowl with one hand and use a fork to cut them one at a time into smaller pieces. If they are served in a cup or footed bowl and placed on a saucer, remove them from the cup and cut them on the saucer—if there is enough room. If they are served with individual sauce bowls, you may dip at will. If the sauce is served from a communal bowl, use a spoon to put the sauce on the shrimp. The same rule holds for any sauce served with any course.

Soaking up with Bread This may be done by breaking off one or two pieces of bread. Place pieces of bread onto a plate or into a soup plate. Spear each piece of bread with a fork, soak up the sauce or juice, and bring it to your mouth with the fork.

Sorbet Sorbet is served between meals to cleanse the palate. It usually is served in some type of stemware. The stemware is held with your thumb and first two fingers on the stem or the base, not the bowl. Scoop the sorbet from side to side moving from right to left side of the stemware bowl. The side of the dish helps to push the sorbet onto the spoon.

Rolls, Biscuits, and Toast

Rolls should be broken with your fingers into moderate-size pieces—one at a time. Butter each piece with your own butter spreader and convey the piece to your mouth.

Biscuits may be split in half with fingers. Place butter or jam on the edge of half of the biscuit with your own breakfast knife or luncheon knife just enough for one bite.

Toast may be broken with your fingers into moderate-size pieces—one at a time. Or you may take bites directly from the slice of toast. Place butter or jam on the edge of toast with your own breakfast knife or luncheon knife just enough for one bite.

Whether you are eating rolls, biscuits, or toast, place butter or jam on the edge of your plate with the serving knife or serving spoon. Place the serving knife or serving spoon back on the serving plate or in the serving bowl.

Do not use the communal serving knife or serving spoon to spread your own butter or jam. Use your own butter spreader, breakfast knife, or luncheon knife to spread your toppings.

When using pats of butter, do not take the butter completely off wrapper— this way you can hold the butter in place with your fingers without getting butter on your hands.

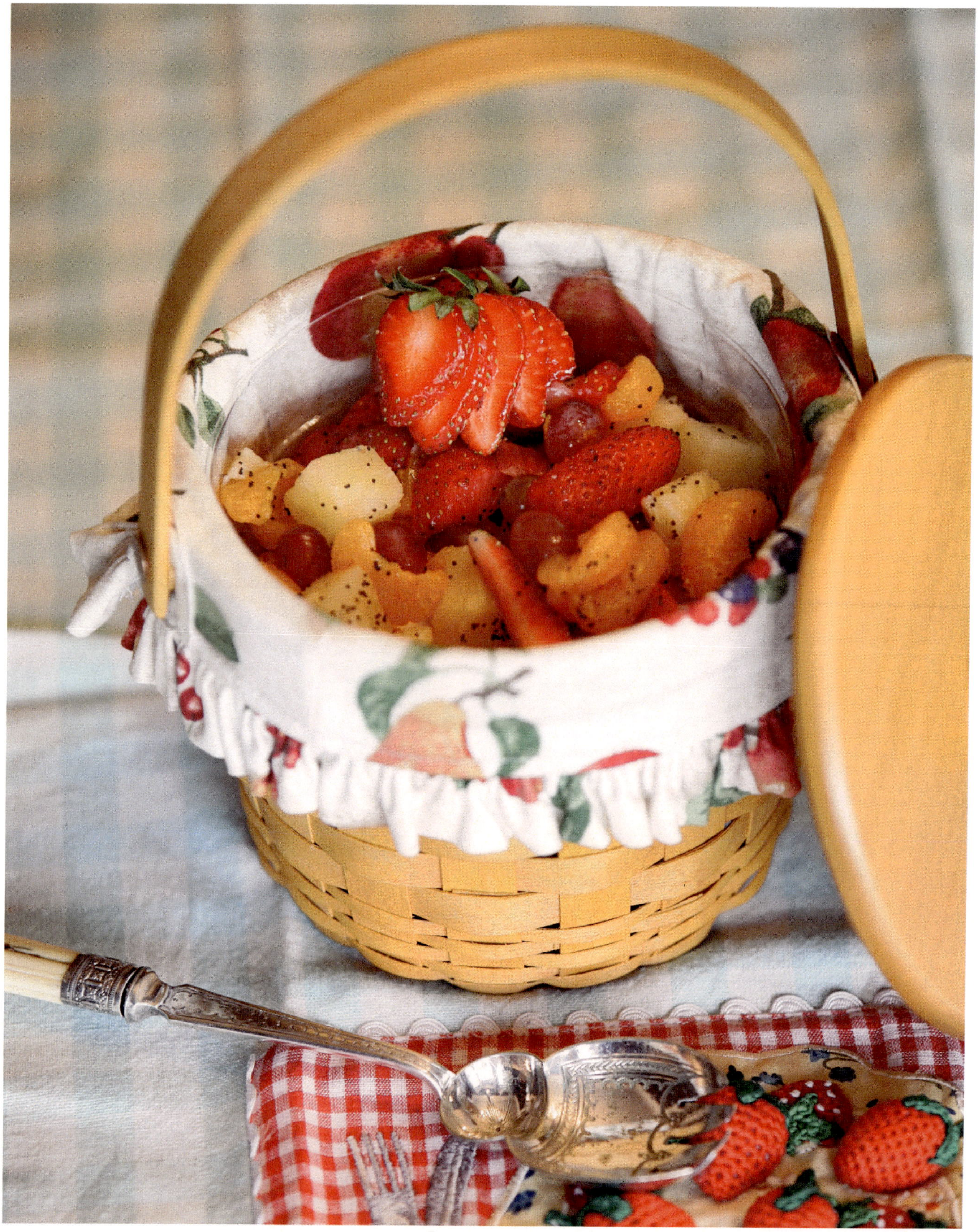

Dining with Fruits

A bowl of fresh fruit often is offered at formal and informal events. In formal events, the fruit will be served on a plate, halved, cored, and cut into smaller sections to eat with a fruit knife and fruit fork. In informal events, some fruits will be cut into quarters. In this case, eat the quarters with a fruit fork. If fruit is served whole, cut and peel the fruit with a fruit knife and eat with a fruit fork.

When you are served canned fruit with pits, clean the pit in your mouth, drop it on a fruit fork, and deposit it on the plate. Listed below are guidelines to assist you in dining with fruits.

Apples and Pears You may use a fruit knife to quarter an apple or pear. This makes it easy to cut out and dispose of the core. You may eat the quartered fruit with a fruit fork. In more formal settings, the fruit is served on a plate, halved, cored, and cut into smaller sections to eat with a fruit knife and fruit fork.

Apricots, Cherries, and Plums These fruits are eaten with your hands, biting as close as you can to the pit. You may put the pit in your mouth. After you have cleaned the pit in your mouth, drop the pit onto a fruit fork and deposit it on the plate. You may also remove the pit from your mouth with your cupped hand and place the pit on the plate.

Bananas Cut ends of banana off with a fruit knife and fruit fork. Proceed to remove entire skin. Cut bite-size pieces, one at a time, and convey each piece into your mouth with a fruit fork.

Berries With the exception of strawberries, most berries are stemmed before serving and eaten with a dessert spoon. Strawberries often are served whole, complete with stems. If so, hold each strawberry by its stem and dip it into powdered sugar or something similar. Take one or two bites and put the stem on the plate.

Cantaloupes and other Melons If served halved, use a dessert spoon to scoop out the flesh. If served in slices and the rind needs to be removed, do so with a fruit knife and fruit fork. Cut and eat a few pieces at a time.

Figs Often served as an appetizer, figs are eaten skin and all with a fruit knife and fruit fork. If served as dessert with a sauce, substitute a dessert spoon instead of a fruit knife and fruit fork. Mature figs, served whole, are halved and eaten with a fruit knife and fruit fork.

Grapefruit Most grapefruit is served sectioned and seeded. Leave the rind and any stray seeds on the plate. The fruit is eaten with a pointed grapefruit spoon or teaspoon.

Grapes Break a sprig of grapes from the bunch or cut off a sprig with grape shears rather than removing one grape at a time. If the grapes contain seeds, remove the seeds from your mouth with your cupped hand and place the seeds on the plate.

Oranges and Tangerines If served whole with the peel, slice off both ends and cut the peel off in vertical strips. You may also easily peel with your fingers. Seeds should be removed with the tip of a fruit knife. A halved orange may also be eaten like a grapefruit.

Mangos Spear the mango with a mango fork, if available, or use a fruit fork. Peel the mango with a fruit knife. After the mango is peeled, secure the mango with a mango fork or a fruit fork and cut away with a mango spoon or dessert spoon. Convey each piece of mango to your mouth with a mango spoon or dessert spoon.

Peaches You may use a fruit knife and cut the peach to the pit, break the peach in half, remove the pit, and then cut it into quarters. You may eat the quarters with a fruit fork. In more formal settings, this fruit is served on a plate, halved and without pits, and eaten with a fruit knife and fruit fork.

Peaches and Pears in Wine or Syrup Peaches and pears in any kind of syrup are eaten Continental style with a dessert spoon and dessert fork. Hold the dessert spoon in your right hand and hold the dessert fork in your left hand with tines facing down. Depending on the style of dining, dessert may be eaten with either utensil. In Continental style of dining, the dessert spoon is used to cut the dessert, while the dessert fork is used to convey dessert to one's mouth. In the English style of dining, the dessert fork serves to push the dessert onto the dessert spoon. The dessert spoon then conveys dessert to one's mouth.

Pineapple A pineapple usually is served already peeled, cored, and sliced in rounds. It is then eaten with a fruit knife and fruit fork.

Persimmons Turn the fruit stem side down and cut it into quarters with a fruit knife. Open each quarter so it lies flat and eat with a fruit knife and fruit fork. This fruit may be halved and eaten with a dessert spoon. Do not eat the bitter skin.

Pomegranates If a pomegranate is served, it is usually halved or served in sections. Extract the seeds carefully with a dessert spoon and eat one or two of the seeds. The seeds are edible—not the membrane. Remember pomegranate juice stains lips, skin, and clothing.

Additional Dining Guidelines

* If you want to rest your arms during the meal, do so by resting your wrists on the edge of the table. There is some history to this old rule. In ancient times, when the fear of a concealed weapon was very common, guests were not allowed to keep their hands on their laps.

* Étiquette dictates that flatware, once used, should never touch the table again.

* All first forks such as cocktail forks, seafood forks, oyster forks, and escargot forks are held in your right hand.

* The proper way to hold a knife and fork is to gently place your forefingers on top of the utensils. This will give you more control when cutting and spearing the food.

* Straws are held with your fingers while drinking.

* When adding salt to your food from a salt cellar, place salt on upper right edge of your plate with a salt spoon. If for some reason there is no salt spoon, use the tip of your clean knife blade to take some. To salt your food, dip food into it. Pepper may be scattered directly on the food since it most likely will be served from a pepper mill. If salt comes in a mill, scatter as you would pepper.

* Never dip your food directly into shared condiment dishes. Condiments usually will be placed on the table with serving utensils that stay with the condiments. Once you have served yourself the condiment on your plate, use a small amount at a time on the food you are eating. A condiment is usually added to the food to complement or enhance the flavor. Do not ask for condiments if they are not on the table.

* You may push food onto your fork inconspicuously with a bit of bread. This may be done when handling difficult foods such as peas. You may also spear a piece of bread with your fork and soak it into a sauce before conveying the piece to your mouth.

* When drinking wine or other liquids from stemware, hold the stemware with your thumb and first two fingers on the stem, not by the bowl. This will prevent the temperature from your hand from interfering with the temperature of the liquid.

* When sipping from a glass or cup, do not look at other guests or look around; lower your eyes into the glass or cup so you can see what you are drinking.

* Never use toothpicks for anything except picking up olives or other small appetizers or hors d'œuvres.

* Never clean your teeth with a toothpick. You may carry your own toothpicks with you and excuse yourself from the dining table and retire to the lavatory to get the offending bit of food out.

* If food is in your teeth and you are unable to dislodge it with your tongue, leave the table and retire to the lavatory to get the bit of food out.

* Speaking with food in your mouth is possible if the amount of food in your mouth is very minimum. If someone directs a question to you and you have food in your mouth, do not reply until most of the food in your mouth has been chewed and eaten first.

* When you must remove something from your mouth either because it has an unpalatable taste or texture, or is impossible to chew, it may be pushed out onto a spoon, fork, paper napkin or even your cupped hands and placed on a plate—never on the table. Do not remove food from your mouth with a cloth napkin. If it is something that was not meant to be eaten (bone, gristle, shell, etc.), place it on the plate without a comment. To make a fuss would embarrass the host or hostess.

* Do not blow your nose at the table. Excuse yourself and go to the lavatory or elsewhere. Be as quiet as possible.

* Bring your fork or spoon to your mouth. Do not lean over your plate or lower your head over your plate.

* Be careful not to raise your flatware in front of another guest's space. Keep it close to your person.

* Do not reach over your guests' plates. Ask to pass the platter or condiment.

There was a fashion in Europe during the nineteenth century for downplaying the knife to such an extent that one was to use it as little as possible but also to put it aside when it was not in use. You cut up your food with the knife in the more capable hand and the fork in the other; you then put down the knife, being careful to place it with the blade's edge towards the center of the plate, not facing your neighbors. Then the fork changed hands and was used to take the cut food to the mouth. More elaborate manners demanded that one should perform this maneuver for every mouthful consumed. Eaters adhering to this fashion thought that people who ate with both hands holding on to the cutlery were gross and coarse. What Emily Post called "zig-zag" eating was still customary among the French bourgeoisie in the eighteen eighties. Branchereau described it as follows: He says, however, the English are successfully introducing a new fashion: they hang on to their knives and take the food to their mouths with the left hand that is still holding the fork! Eating in the "English" manner means the fork, having just left off being an impaling instrument, must enter the mouth with the tines down if it is not to be awkwardly swiveled round in the left, or less capable, hand. Food, therefore, must be balanced on the back of the rounded tines.

Your Professional Life

First impressions are extremely important. Manners at home, work, or social events are the basis for getting along in all aspects of our lives. Whether meeting new people at a social event, shaking hands at a dinner or business function, answering the telephone, or writing personal and business letters, one must demonstrate proper etiquette.

The étiquette of communication is very important. One of the most important communication methods is eye contact. As you meet new people at work or socialize in restaurants or other events, engage the conversation with attentive eye contact.

Listening is also a very important skill. Do not fidget. Show interest in the conversation by asking questions.

Body language shows your level of self-confidence. Keep good posture whether you are sitting or standing. Keep your arms loosely at your sides in a fluid position with your right hand free for shaking hands or holding a drink.

Be polite and courteous on the telephone. Take messages in a professional manner. Ask for first and last names. Ask for a phone number. Write down the date and the time the call was received. Make sure the message gets to the correct person.

When calling a friend or colleague at home, good telephone manners dictate not to call before 9 o'clock in the morning or after 9 o'clock in the evening.

If someone calls your parents, brother, or sister, or anyone who lives in your home: Say, "Hold on; I will see if he/she is available." Or, "I'm sorry he/she is not available." Followed by, "May I have your name and number in order to leave a message?" Calls should be returned before twenty-four hours.

Ideally, call waiting only should be used if you are expecting an important call. If you have call waiting and receive a call during a conversation, never disconnect with the person to whom you are speaking. Ask the person you are speaking with to hold for a moment. Inform the person calling that you are on the telephone and will return the call.

Emailing and texting are great ways to communicate. Try to get back to people in a timely manner. Do not assume people enjoy forwarded emails; check with them before sending.

Respect the privacy and the boundaries of your co-workers. Do not read their mail or office memos. Do not give unsolicited opinions; people will ask for your advice if it is wanted. Always knock on someone's office door before entering. Return things that you borrow. Refrain from smoking in the office. Clean up after yourself in the break room. Respect and be considerate of others' views.

Always present and receive business cards using both hands. Hold the cards on the top portion of the card. Make a point when you have received someone's card to review it and comment on it before putting it away.

In the business world as is the case elsewhere, good manners and consideration for others are timeless. Recognize this and you will have good friends and business associates and, most importantly, you will be at ease in any situation.

Office Romance The practice of office romances used to be frowned upon and, in many cases, became the cause for dismissal from companies. Today, this rule is not as strict as it once was. However, most employers are interested in their employees concentrating on their work and not on their co-workers. An office romance may, and often does, lead to distraction. Therefore, if you become interested in a fellow worker, try to be as discreet as possible. Don't take advantage of situations which could possibly generate office gossip. If you choose to date a fellow worker and the relationship ends, you might feel awkward around that individual in the day-to-day workplace. If the breakup indeed does become painful, you may even find yourself looking for another job.

Prayer in the Office Although you might do a lot of praying in the hope of finishing a project on time, limit this to yourself unless you have a clear understanding with your co-workers. Prayer is a very private matter and everyone seems to have a different opinion of it and its place. Some companies may even sponsor voluntary prayer groups, but this only works if the employees feel no corporate pressure to attend such a group.

Office Parties When invited to an office party, you have the option to attend or to not attend. If you can attend, inform your boss. If you cannot attend, regretfully inform your boss. Office politics being what they are, it's often the person who is most visible, both during and after hours, who gets the promotion. This visibility demonstrates that, no matter the time or no matter the day, you are available for the company. There are definitely pros and cons with office parties; so be sure to make up your own mind about them. Your behavior should be impeccable. A good idea is to plan to attend the function for a short period. This way you have the option to leave or stay. By doing this, you won't feel manipulated or trapped.

It's Possible to Be Friends The overall rule in business étiquette and corporate courtesies is to carve out a niche for yourself while simultaneously working within the structure of the company. It definitely is important to retain your individualism; yet you must remember that the moment you enter the office workplace, you are part of a diverse and skilled team. The same social graces that apply to general life also apply here. Be conscientious and respectful of others. Be kind, courteous, and sincere. Do these things and you will find that your life, both personally and professionally, will be rewarded beyond words.

When you Disagree Carefully show respect for others and yourself. Be honest and state your opinion. You may use words like, "In my opinion…" which is quite diplomatic. You may agree to disagree without being critical. Remain calm and do not pursue the topic if it becomes heated.

Virtues

FROM THE BOOK OF VIRTUES
A TREASURY OF GREAT MORAL STORIES
BY
WILLIAM J. BENNETT

Virtues are traits and values deemed to be morally valued and are the foundations and characteristics promoting individual greatness. If practiced daily, one can achieve a good life. Listed below and in the following pages are some important virtues for well being and happiness. Though written many years ago, most are appropriate even today.

Self-Discipline

George Washington
Rules of Civility and Decent Behavior

The first eight virtues

Every action in company ought to be with some sign of respect to those present.

In the presence of others sing not to yourself with a humming voice,
nor drum with your fingers or feet.

Speak not when others speak, sit not when others stand,
and walk not when others stop.

Turn not your back to others, especially in speaking; jog not the table or desk on which
another reads or writes; lean not on anyone.

Be no flatterer, neither play with anyone that delights not to be played with.

Read no letters, books, or papers in company; but when there is a necessity for doing it, you
must ask leave. Come not near the books or writings of anyone so as to read them unasked;
also look not nigh when another is writing a letter.

Let your countenance be pleasant, but in serious matters somewhat grave.

Show not yourself glad at the misfortune of another, though he were your enemy.

Compassion

Kindness to Animals

Little children, never give
Pain to things that feel and live;
Let the gentle robin come
For the crumbs you save at home;
As his meat you throw along
He'll repay you with a song.
Never hurt the timid hare
Peeping from her green grass lair,
Let her come and sport and play
On the lawn at close of day.
The little lark goes soaring high
To the bright windows of the sky,
Singing as if 'twere always spring,
And fluttering on an untried wing -
Oh! let him sing his happy song,
Nor do these gentle creatures wrong.

Responsibility

Thomas Jefferson
The Declaration of Independence

When in the Course of human events, it becomes necessary for one people to dissolve the political bands which have connected them with another, and to assume among the Powers of the earth, the separate and equal station to which the Laws of Nature and of Nature's God entitle them, a decent respect to the opinions of mankind requires that they should declare the causes which impel them to the separation. — We hold these truths to be self-evident, that all men are created equal, that they are endowed by their Creator with certain unalienable Rights, that among these are Life, Liberty and the pursuit of Happiness. — That to secure these rights, Governments are instituted among Men, deriving their just powers from the consent of the governed, — That whenever any Form of Government becomes destructive of these ends, it is the Right of the People to alter or to abolish it, and to institute new Government, laying its foundation on such principles and organizing its powers in such form, as to them shall seem most likely to effect their Safety and Happiness.

Friendship

Poem

Friendship needs no studied phrases,
Polished face, or winning wiles;
Friendship deals no lavish praises,
Friendship dons no surface smiles.

Friendship follows Nature's diction,
Shuns the blandishments of art,
Boldly severs truth from fiction,
Speaks the language of the heart.

Friendship favors no condition,
Scorns a narrow-minded creed,
Lovingly fulfills its mission,
Be it word or be it deed.

Friendship cheers the faint and weary,
Makes the timid spirit brave,
Warns the erring, lights the dreary,
Smooths the passage to the grave.

Friendship—pure, unselfish friendship,
All through life's allotted span,
Nurtures, strengthens, widens, lengthens,
Man's relationship with man.

Work

Ralph Waldo Emerson
Great Men

Not gold, but only man can make
A people great and strong;
Men who, for truth and honor's sake,
Stand fast and suffer long.
Brave men who work while other sleep,
Who dare while others fly—
They build a nation's pillars deep
And lift them to the sky.

Honesty

Ben Jonson
Truth

Truth is the trial of itself,
And needs no other touch;
And purer than the purest gold,
Refine it ne'er so much.
It is the life and light of love,
The sun that ever shineth,
And spirit of that special grace,
That faith and love defineth.
It is the warrant of the word,
That yields a scent so sweet,
As gives a power to faith to tread
All falsehood under feet.

Perseverance

Abraham Lincoln
The Gettysburg Address

Four score and seven years ago, our fathers brought forth on this continent a new nation, conceived in liberty, and dedicated to the proposition that all men are created equal. Now we are engaged in a great civil war, testing whether that nation, or any nation so conceived and so dedicated, can long endure. We are met on a great battlefield of that war. We have come to dedicate a portion of that field as a final resting place for those who here gave their lives that that nation might live. It is altogether fitting and proper that we should do this. But in a larger sense we cannot dedicate, we cannot consecrate, we cannot hallow this ground. The brave men, living and dead, who struggled here, have consecrated it far above our poor power to add or detract. The world will little note, nor long remember, what we say here, but it can never forget what they did here. It is for us the living, rather, to be dedicated here to the unfinished work which they who fought here have thus far so nobly advanced. It is rather for us to be here dedicated to the great task remaining before us—that from these honored dead we take increased devotion to that cause for which they gave the last full measure of devotion, that we here highly resolve that these dead shall not have died in vain, that this nation, under God, shall have a new birth of freedom, and that government of the people, by the people, for the people, shall not perish from the earth.

Appropriate Dress Attire

A sure sign of successful étiquette is dressing appropriately.

Woman's Dress Attire

Formal (White Tie) White tie dress for women is often a full-skirted dress that is suitable for dancing. Its length should not quite reach the floor with shoes on. Additional formal wear includes long, elbow-length gloves, shoes with heels, and appropriate jewelry.

Formal (Black Tie) A woman may choose between a cocktail dress, a dinner suit of street length, or a long, formal evening dress for this affair. Gloves may be worn. Shoes with heels should be worn.

Semi-Formal Semi-formal indicates a mid-length dress or gown, appropriate shoes, and a shoulder wrap if desired. Your attire should be elegant but not as regimented as black or white tie.

Informal Informal dress means to dress nicely in a mid-length dress or pant suit with appropriate shoes.

Business A mid-length dress or pant suit is appropriate. Suits with jackets are also appropriate. Dark shoes are preferred.

Casual The key to this category is to dress appropriately for the occasion so as to fit in with other invitees.

Man's Dress Attire

Formal White Tie White tie includes a white tie, a winged collar, a tailcoat, black trousers and socks, and plain black shoes. This type of dress rarely is requested today except for very special formal events.

Formal Black Tie This is the most popular and common of the formal dress codes. If the invitation does not specify a dress code, you should assume it is formal black tie. Some of the choices are single- or double-breasted black jacket with black pants (with satin or grosgrain faille down the outside leg seam), black shoes and black dress socks, a white dress shirt (front pleated or tuxedo), a waistcoat or cummerbund, and a dressy silk or satin bow tie.

Semi-Formal Appropriate semi-formal includes a white jacket, dark trousers, a bow tie, a pleated or ruffled shirt, a cummerbund, and black shoes. Patterns or colors for the bow tie and cummerbund are appropriate.

Business This is a suit with a dress shirt, a full-length tie, dark socks, and black shoes.

Informal or Casual Any outfit that is appropriate for business attire is appropriate here. In addition, you may choose to dress in nice slacks, a sport jacket, dress shirt, dark socks, and dark shoes. A tie is optional but still preferred in certain social circles.

Memorial Day is the beginning of warm weather and the tradition of wearing white begins. This custom continues until Labor Day, at which point it becomes one of the most common and most easily spotted faux pas in the American tradition. If you live in the South, most people are probably aware of this custom and, therefore, it is a breach of étiquette if the rule is violated.

In the past, formal attire for men and women were never worn before six o'clock in the evening. If the function began in the afternoon, the host would have provided a place where the guests could dress for the formal evening.

Remember – gentlemen never wear their hats indoors!

Tiaras are only worn by married women. Gloves should be worn at all times except when dining at which point they should be removed and placed on the lap underneath the napkin.

Personal Grooming

Personal grooming is one of the most important rules of étiquette. Putting your best foot forward is very important and that means being clean and odor free. Body odors, bad breath, dirty fingernails, and greasy hair can push people away and keep you from being invited out or invited to people's homes.

Always wash your hands before sitting down to a meal or serving a meal. Bathe and shower daily. Keep your hair clean. Wash it every day or every other day and do not play with it at the dining table. Brush your teeth in the morning and in the evening. Clean your clothes regularly.

These are just a few daily rituals that are designed to go hand-in-hand with good manners.

Dear Lady Bernadette:

We attended your etiquette talk at the NW Tea Festival and really enjoyed the time with you. Our society needs your instruction now more than ever and "the art of the social graces" should be required education for all.

We thank you sincerely!
Debbie & Tracy

Thank-you note sent to me after teaching a Tea Étiquette Class.

Thank-You Notes

hank-you notes are usually the most enjoyable to write. For some of us, however, the tricky part is writing them before too much time has gone by; the longer we wait to respond, the more difficult it becomes to express our thanks with freshness and sincerity. It is best to send them out as soon as possible so they are not forgotten in all of the excitement of the occasion. Generally, thank-you notes should be sent out within a week of receipt of a gift or gesture. Some exceptions are as follows:

- Thank-you notes to a hostess for a dinner or tea should be sent within twenty-four hours. You may also send flowers along with your note of thanks.
- Answering condolence letters should be six to eight weeks after the funeral.
- A bride and groom should send thank-you notes for wedding presents within three weeks. However, if the task proves monumental, it may be extended for up to three months.

Sample Thank-You Note

Dear John and Sue,

I can't remember when Joe and I had a better time than at your new home last night. You both did a spectacular job with the seafood pasta and we were delighted to visit with your son Christopher. I only hope we did not stay too long. Thank you John and Sue for including us.

        All the best to you both,

        Joe and Mary

Around the eighteen hundreds when tea was very expensive and kept in locked containers called tea caddy boxes, special tea caddy spoons were designed and kept in them. In the early eighteen hundreds tea caddy spoons were given as gifts and were often engraved for special purposes.

History of Tea

An old legend credits the Chinese Emperor Shen Nung in the twenty-eighth century BC with the discovery of tea. As the story is told, the health-conscious emperor knew that boiling water before drinking seemed to protect people from disease. He always insisted on having his water boiled and that simple precaution led to a wonderful revelation. One day while touring the provinces, the Emperor stopped for a rest with his entourage. Servants gathered branches from a nearby evergreen bush to build a fire for boiling the Emperor's water. A passing wind blew leaves from the bush into the boiling pot and soon a delightful aroma issued forth. Intrigued, the Emperor quickly sipped a bit of the infusion. He immediately declared that the refreshing brew must have medicinal qualities and ordered his servants to gather leaves from the bush to take back to the palace.

News of the Emperor's discovery spread quickly throughout the provinces. Soon everyone in China was drinking tea and the infusion of that evergreen plant quickly became an important part of the Chinese culture. Over the centuries the knowledge and appreciation of tea gradually spread to other parts of the Orient.

After hundreds and hundreds of years, tea finally arrived in England and by 1660 tea was flowing everywhere on the island. One Samuel Pepys, renowned seventeenth-century diarist, noted in 1660 that he had his very first "cup of tee of which I had never drunk before." In 1662, when England's King Charles II married Portugal's Princess Catherine of Braganza, part of her dowry was a chest of tea. It was this Queen's love for tea and her influence on the royal court that influenced the spread of the "new drink." Tea merchants soon were offering tea as an elixir for just about anything that ailed anyone. It was first served in public coffeehouses and in outdoor "tea gardens" then increasingly served in homes.

Around 1650, Dutch ships carrying the new drink to the Dutch colony of New Amsterdam introduced it to the American colony. It took another twenty years for the rest of the colonies to become acquainted with tea, though no one really had any idea of how to use it properly. Americans would let the tea brew and stew for hours creating a dark bitter drink. They also salted and ate the used leaves on buttered bread. It wasn't until 1674 when the British took over New Amsterdam and renamed it New York that the custom of tea drinking as we now know it began.

Tea was enjoyed in the American Colonies until the late eighteenth century. However, when King George III decided to use tea as a source of revenue and raised the import tax on tea sent to the Colonies, the independent-minded Americans rebelled. In 1773, the colonists dressed as Native Americans and dumped a shipload of tea into the Boston Harbor. This event became known as the Boston Tea Party and was one of many that propelled the Colonies toward independence and probably indirectly led to a marked preference for coffee in the United States.

Around 1840, the custom of Afternoon Tea began in England and is credited to one of Queen Victoria's ladies-in-waiting, Anna Maria Stanhope, known as the Duchess of Bedford. In England at the time, people ate a heavy breakfast, a late dinner, and very little in between. Toward midafternoon the Duchess routinely experienced a "sinking feeling" which she remedied by dining in her boudoir with tea, cakes, tarts, and biscuits. Others soon followed the Duchess' lead and in a few decades the custom of "taking tea" in the afternoon became well established. At first the practice was limited to the upper classes, but it eventually became so popular that tea shops and tearooms began opening for the enjoyment of the general public. This elegant custom became popularized greatly during the height of the Victorian Era making "teatime" a regular pastime of the proper English Lady.

By the late nineteenth century, teatime had acquired its own formal étiquette. Tea services were made of silver or china. Fine linens were used for tea cloths and serviettes (table napkins). Tea gowns were loose and flowing with matching hats and gloves. The tea itself was imported from India or Ceylon (now Sri Lanka)—colonies of the British Empire. With the tea came decorated platters of savories (dainty finger sandwiches), scones with jams or homemade preserves and clotted cream, toast with cinnamon, petits fours (small cakes cut from pound or sponge cakes and frosted), and other delicacies that came to be known as "tea food." In working class homes, Afternoon Tea became a much heartier affair with cold meats, cheeses, and breads. This evening meal was called "high tea" and often replaced dinner.

The United States can claim two distinct contributions when it comes to tea, both dating from the twentieth century. In 1904, visitors to the Louisiana Purchase Exposition in St. Louis sweltered in a heat wave and shunned the hot brew offered by Indian tea growers. An Englishman named Richard Blechynden, who represented the tea growers, experimented with pouring the tea over ice in order to entice fair visitors. The result was a success. Iced tea now accounts for eighty percent of the tea drunk in the United States. The second contribution is the tea bag, the brainstorm of an American tea merchant named Thomas Sullivan, who hit on the idea of providing samples to his customers in small silk pouches or "a tea-leaf holder." Sullivan's customers soon discovered that the pouches could be put directly in teapots. Orders came pouring in for the tea packaged in those little bags and Sullivan patented his brainstorm.

Nearly five thousand years have gone by since Emperor Shen Nung sipped the first cup of tea on that Chinese roadside and almost two centuries have elapsed since the Duchess of Bedford first thought of tea and cakes to carry her through until dinnertime. So much time has passed yet some things do grow better with age. Tea may be enjoyed today with a sense of history and a sense of kinship with those who made significant contributions to the development of this lovely pastime.

English-style tea places the loose leaves in a pot and pours the brewed tea through a tea strainer into a teacup. Be warned—the second cup of tea may be over brewed and bitter.

Influences in the World of Tea

Catherine of Braganza

atherine arrived in Portsmouth on May 13, 1662, for her arranged marriage to King Charles II of England. It had been a long and stormy crossing. She immediately asked for a cup of tea and was offered a glass of ale instead. Not surprisingly, she retired to her bedchamber with illness. Within a very short time, she married the King and with her came her dowry which included a great deal of money, territories of Tangier and Bombay, luxury gifts, and a chest of tea, the favorite drink at the Portuguese court.

Queen Anne of England

Reigned 1702 to 1714
Enjoyed tea with her morning meal in a time when very heavy alcoholic beverages were the drinks of choice.

Anna Maria

Originator of Afternoon Tea
Duchess of Bedford and one of Queen Victoria's ladies-in-waiting.
The Duchess found that a light meal of tea and cakes was the perfect balance to fill the midday gap between meals. She began to invite her friends to join her, and soon Afternoon Tea quickly became an established repast in middle-class and upper-class households.

Queen Victoria of England

Reigned 1837 to 1901
The Queen was very enthusiastic about Afternoon Tea and endorsed this leisure activity believing it would be good for her nation's economy and would enhance social skills. She hosted fancy tea parties and even baked sweets for her Prince Consort.

The habit of putting cream in tea reportedly started in France. The French were enjoying tea long before the beverage found its way to the wealthy homes of London. Madame de Sevigne described how Madame de la Sablière launched the fashion—Madame de la Sablière took her tea with cream, as she told me the other day, because it was to her taste.

Afternoon Tea in England

From the Home of Jane Austen

Anna, the seventh Duchess of Bedford (1783-1857), is credited with originating Afternoon Tea in England. This charming custom grew out of very practical necessity. In those days in England people ate a heavy breakfast, a late dinner, and very little in between. Toward mid-afternoon the Duchess routinely experienced a "sinking feeling" that she remedied by dining in her boudoir on tea, cakes, tarts, and biscuits at about four in the afternoon.

The typical "tea and toast" breakfast that Jane Austen (1775-1817) enjoyed was a relatively new invention. Traditionally, British breakfasts had consisted of a hearty fare that often included beef and ale. By the end of the eighteenth century, however, many people, especially those of the upper classes, considered such breakfasts to be antiquated and rustic. In the early seventeen hundreds Queen Anne first set the mode of drinking tea for her morning meal, preferring the light, refreshing drink to the heavy, alcoholic beverages that were usually taken in the morning.

At what time people took their evening tea was a matter of personal preference because it generally followed the end of dinner by one or two hours—thus teatime depended on when dinner was eaten. When Jane Austen's parents were young, dining in the early to middle afternoon was usual. People of fashion, to distinguish themselves from the common folk, dined later, perhaps three or four o'clock. Naturally, aspiring ladies and gentlemen changed their hours to imitate high society which responded by pushing the dinner hour even later. A little dance ensued, with the upper classes and the stylish retreating from the dreadful fate of being thought common, and the would-be fashionable following as fast as they could.

By the Regency period the modish were dining at six o'clock, or seven o'clock, or even later. The Austens themselves altered their dinnertime over the years as the fashion changed. In 1798, Jane jokingly wrote to her sister, Cassandra, who was staying at their wealthy brother's house, "We dine now a half after three and have done dinner I suppose before you begin. We drink tea a half after six. I am afraid you will despise us." But in 1808 she noted, "We never dine now till five." The modern practice of having "Afternoon Tea" before dinner probably would have struck Jane Austen and her contemporaries as odd. In her era tea was always served after dinner. The custom in England during the Georgian and Regency periods was for the ladies to withdraw after dinner. The gentlemen lingered in the dining room indulging in wine and presumably in free and easy male conversation. In the drawing room the ladies talked, read, or worked on stitchery to pass the time until the men joined them after an hour or so for tea.

Also, during this time, Richard Twining estimated that at least half the tea drunk in England was smuggled; almost everyone, it seemed—even clergymen—bought smuggled tea. Why, then, did some families choose to buy the more expensive, legally imported tea? The answers were easy—for the taste and quality. To keep sea water out of it on the crossing to England, smuggled tea was packed in large oilskin bags which gave it an off taste. On landing, the tea was usually repacked in sacks which were then slung over horses for the trip inland. Add horse sweat to the lingering flavor of oilskin and you get an idea of why many people preferred the taste of legal tea.

There was another reason to purchase legal tea. Housemaids could earn a nice income by drying their employers' soggy used tea leaves and selling them out the back door to unscrupulous dealers. The leaves were dyed to look new and resold to unwary buyers. The quality was perhaps stretched with the addition of other leaves, twigs, and sometimes floor sweepings. Even worse, an illegal industry sprang up to manufacture a type of bogus tea called "smouch" that never saw China in its life. According to Richard Twining, who led the fight against the adulteration of tea, the fake tea was made with ash tree leaves that were dried, baked, trod upon until the leaves were small, then lifted and steeped in copperas with sheep's dung, after which they were dried on a floor. Copperas is another name for green vitriol, a toxic substance used to make black dye and ink to tan leather and to manufacture gunpowder.

Flowers add much beauty to a tea table. According to flower étiquette, a guest should not bring flowers for the host or hostess as they, as well as the house staff, would be too occupied with the arrangements of the tea to accept them. It might be a better idea to call a few days before the event and suggest that you would like to send flowers for the occasion and note the favorites and color preferences.

114

Styles of Tea

Styles of tea developed depending on people's daily activities. There is no doubt that sometime between the late 1830s and early 1840s, the taking of tea in the afternoon developed into a new social event that filled the refreshment gap between luncheon at noon and dinner around 8:00 PM. In our modern society today tea times evolve and progress and continue to fill our daily lives with tranquility and serenity.

Below are various forms of enjoying this favorite beverage.

High Tea In the past High Tea was considered the tea of peasants and farmers rather than the tea of the elite. This tea was a hearty affair. Meat pies, Welsh rarebit, shepherd's pies, slices of roast, sausage, vegetables, casseroles, puddings, heavy desserts, and other dinnertime staples usually made with leftovers commonly were served. The term "High" came about because the tea meal was taken at a high dining table or with high-back chairs all around a table. This was to distinguish the meal from the Afternoon Tea that was taken at low tables. In recent years, High Tea has become a term for elaborate Afternoon Tea, though this is an American usage and mainly unrecognized in Britain. A proper High Tea is usually served between 5:00 PM and 8:00 PM.

High Tea is sometimes confused with the teas that King Edward VII hosted during his reign from 1901 to 1910. The King, it seems, had so many meals in his daily schedule that he had to change everyone else's schedules also. Dinnertime was pushed forward another hour or so to 8:30 PM or 9:00 PM so that High Tea could now be held even later in the afternoon, bringing it to what most Americans think of as dinnertime around 5:00 PM or later. Known for his huge appetite, the King ate no less than twelve courses at dinner and is responsible for adding "appetizers" to the dinner menus of the British society.

Formal Afternoon Tea Formal Afternoon Tea is an elaborate affair with white linen tablecloths, silver teapots, bone china, and several different types of tea. Darjeeling and Ceylon varieties are suggested for this teatime. Tea fare consists of scones, at least four varieties of savories, and beautiful finger desserts or petits fours presented on three-tiered racks often buffet style. Traditional service time is 4:00 PM. However, any time between 2:00 PM and 5:00 PM is appropriate.

Afternoon Tea or Low Tea Afternoon Tea or Low Tea is designed to enhance social skills and is usually served in fine fashion and in several courses. The term "Low Tea" may come from the fact that hotels traditionally have used low tables in their lobbies to hold the foods and tea service presented at Afternoon Teas. This full tea service includes scones, savories, and a variety of petits fours. It is traditionally served at 4:00 PM; however, any time between 2:00 PM and 5:00 PM is appropriate.

Special Event or Seasonal Tea This tea is designed for the season, occasion, or personal style for the hostess or honored guest. Although this tea requires planning, it also provides an opportunity for creativity in theme, menus, table settings, favors, and invitations. Examples include bridal teas, sweetheart teas, Christmas teas, harvest teas, baby shower teas, business teas, retirement teas, graduation teas, garden teas, and benefit teas.

Cream Tea Cream Tea basically is an afternoon sweet-tooth tea that features a heavy clotted cream from Devonshire. The term "cream" applies to the clotted cream rather than putting cream in the tea. Cream is too rich to accompany tea as it will curdle; milk is the preferred addition. Besides scones this tea includes fresh fruits, berries in season, and cake. Cream Tea is traditionally served from 1:00 PM to 4:00 PM.

Brunch Tea Brunch Tea is a hearty tea to start one's day with a warm egg dish, fresh fruit, or pastries light on sugar content. This is the perfect time to seek a hearty breakfast tea since the traditional time is from 10:00 AM to 1:00 PM.

Teddy Bear Tea This special tea, really hot chocolate, was prepared by nannies for their young charges. The children would scurry off to their quarters to play with their favorite dolls or bears and sip hot chocolate while munching on goodies from the adults' tea table.

The "Elevenses" The term "Elevenses" came from the British and was their version of the American office coffee break between 10:00 AM and 11:00 AM in the morning. In Britain, a tea cart with tea, crumpets, scones, or cinnamon toast was wheeled in for the break.

Remember one drinks tea—one does not take tea. During the Victorian era, the term to take tea was used by the lower classes and considered a vulgar expression by the upper classes.

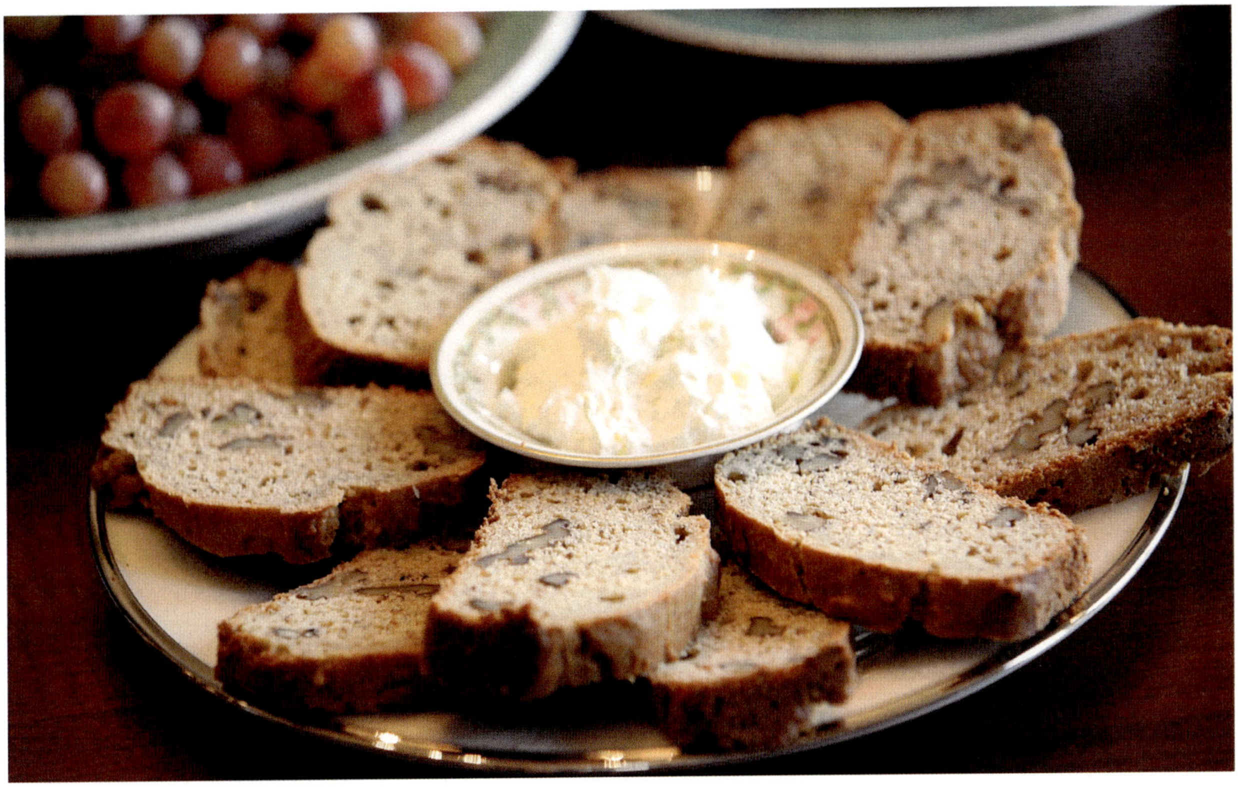

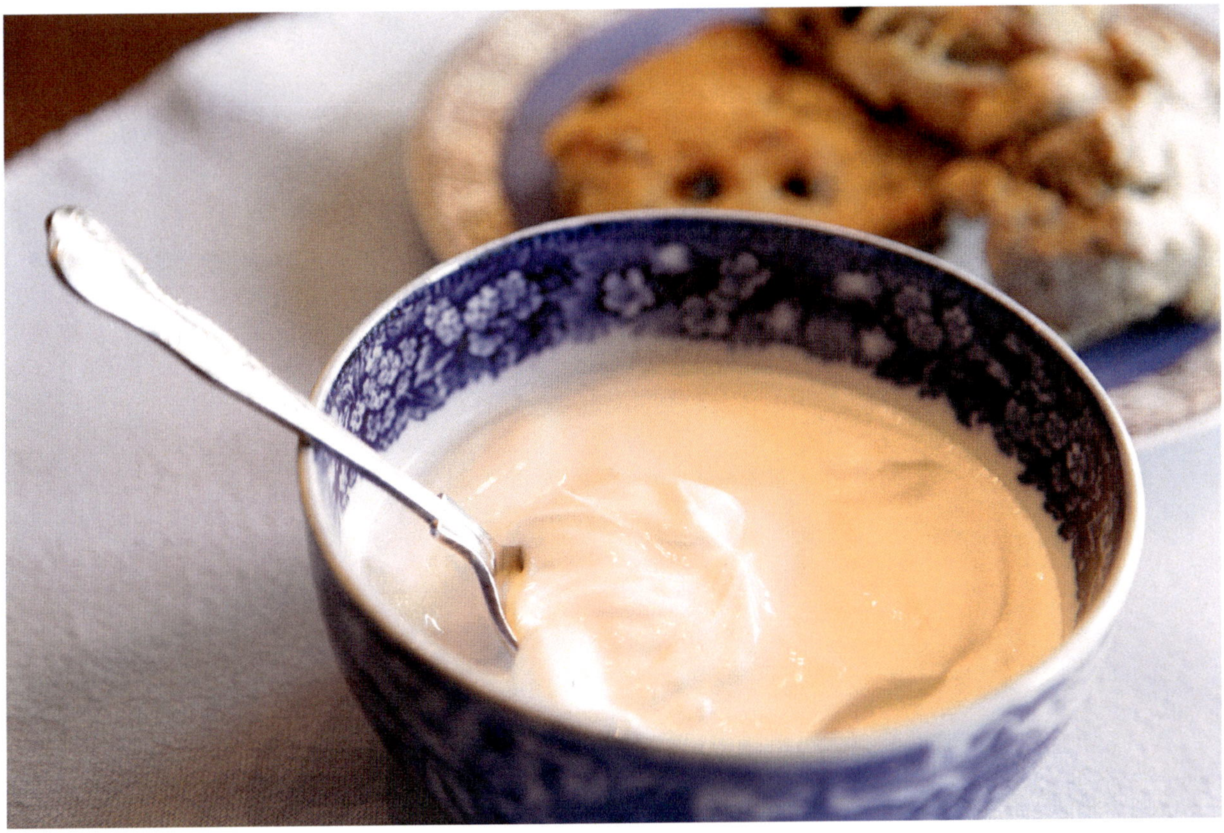

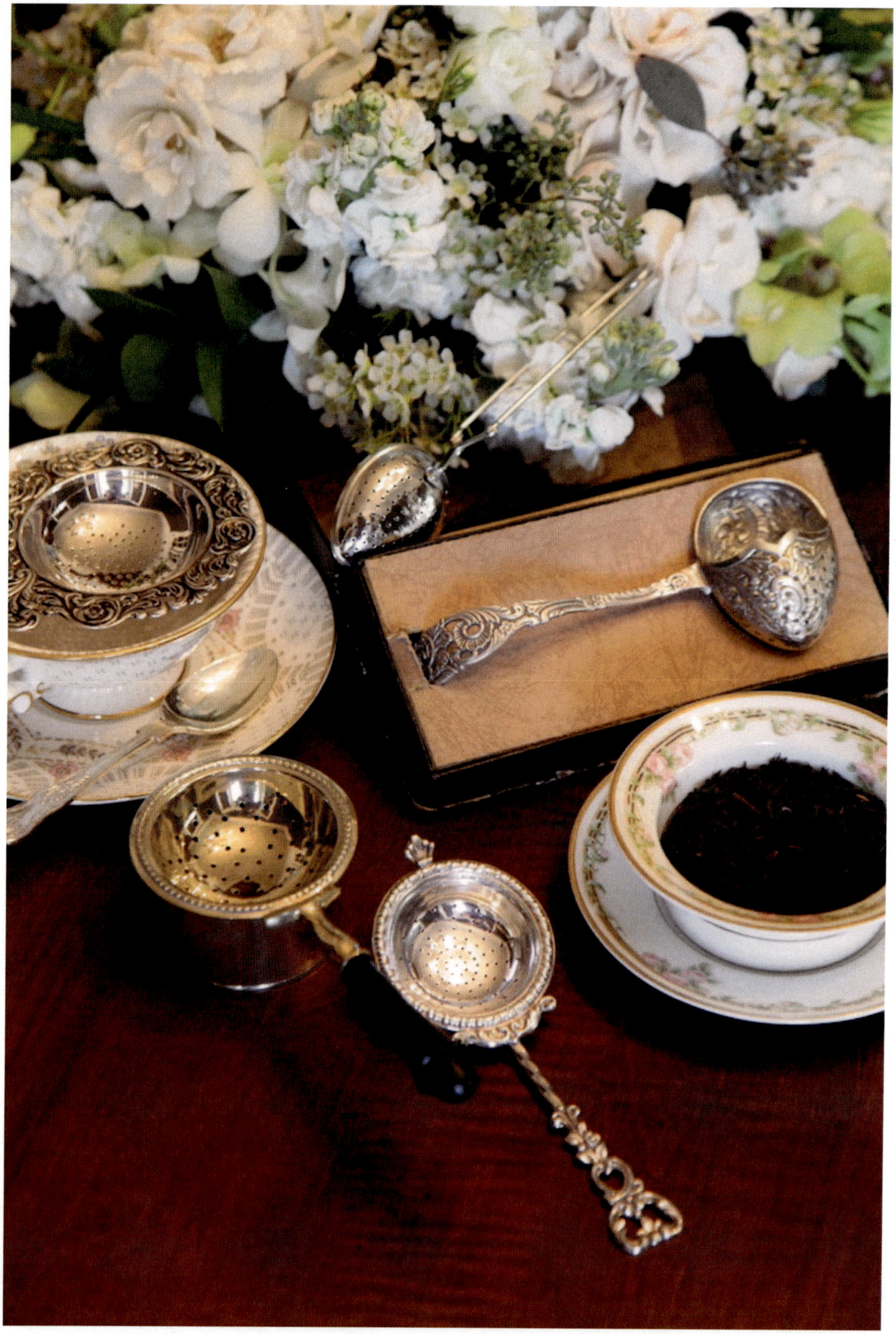

Camellia Sinensis

Camellia Sinensis is an evergreen bush. All teas come from this single source.

Today two main varieties of the tea plant are recognized. One is Camellia Sinensis Sinensis, the Chinese multiple-stem shrub with small leaves, which is long lived and can withstand cold weather. The other is Camellia Sinensis Assamica, the Indian single-stem plant with larger, softer leaves—more like a tree if left unpruned. This is more delicate, shorter lived, and best grown in subtropical and rainy regions.

In terms of the history of tea-drinking practices, we can distinguish three main phases: boiled, whisked, and steeped. The earliest form of tea drinking that is still practiced today in Central Asia and Tibet is boiled tea—usually made with compressed tea that is shaved off a brick or broken off a cake and allowed to boil with the water for a while—sometimes along with other ingredients.

By the tenth century, during the Song Dynasty (960-1279), whisked tea became popular in China. This is the tea that traveled to Japan and was incorporated into ceremonial practices. Tea leaves were ground into a fine powder and whipped with bamboo whisks and hot water in individual bowls.

It was only during the Ming Dynasty (1368-1644) that steeped tea (tea leaves allowed to steep in the teapot) became common practice in China. This is the tea that maritime traders, the Portuguese and the Dutch, first brought to Europe during the seventeenth century.

Teas are often named after the region in which they are grown, such as Assam or Ceylon. The levels of caffeine vary in different teas. This is thought to depend on the age of the leaf, when it is plucked, its location on the stem, the length of oxidation time, the size of the tea leaves brewed, and the quantity of leaf used to make the brew. Tea has more caffeine per dry weight than coffee, but it takes far less tea to make a cup of tea than coffee beans to make a cup of coffee. If you make green tea, you usually use less tea. Hence, there is less caffeine in green tea. About 75% to 80% of the available caffeine in the tea leaves will have come into the solution in the first 60-90 seconds of brewing. The tea leaf is processed into many types of tea. Tea leaves are either used singly or mixed with other leaves to form a blend. The combinations are endless.

120

Types of Tea

White Tea White tea is named after the tiny white or silver hairs that cover the bud as it develops at the tip of each tea shoot. The teas usually are made from just the unopened bud. This is the least processed of all teas. After picking, leaves are left to dry in the sun or in a warm drying room. Leaf buds are withered in bamboo baskets and sometimes placed over a charcoal fire to eliminate most of the remaining moisture. White tea has the highest antioxidant levels and lowest caffeine content of all tea types.

Types: Silver Needle, White Peony, and White Darjeeling.

Yellow Tea Yellow tea is China's rarest. Similar to white teas, it is made from the skillfully picked new buds which are then piled and left so that the heat generated from the natural oxidation process dries them out and prevents any further decomposition. The warm leaves are wrapped in cow skin paper and allowed to dry naturally which gives the yellow color.

Green Tea Green tea is not oxidized at all. The leaves are steamed after picking to prevent fermentation. Green tea has very high antioxidants, polyphenols, and chlorophyll. These leaves produce a delicate brew that is very light in color. Mothers have used green tea for centuries to help upset stomachs and there is increasing medical evidence that drinking green tea provides unsuspected health benefits.

Types: Sencha, Bancha, Matcha, and Gunpowder.

Oolong Tea Oolong tea is a compromise between black and green teas. Fresh shoots with one new bud and three leaves are gathered as they reach their peak on the bush and immediately are processed. It is partially oxidized tea with leaves that are greenish black. The leaves are turned every two hours to cause bruising. When oxidation level has reached about 70%, the leaves are then dried in hot ovens. All oolongs have a naturally occurring fragrance described as an orchid. The brew produced is lighter in both flavor and color. Oolong teas contain more caffeine than green teas but less than black teas.

Black Tea Black tea is completely oxidized which is achieved by withering, rolling, oxidizing, and finally firing the leaves. Black teas produce rich and hearty brews that are very popular. They are shelf-stable teas that became very important during long journeys by ships from Canton to London and ports in between. Fresh green leaves were also shipped but became moldy.

White tea is sundried and picked in early spring.
The unopened buds are covered with white down.
Green tea is in the natural state then fired.
Yellow tea is also used in the natural state but is fired after one day.
Oolong tea is not fully oxidized.
Black tea is completely oxidized.
In essence, white tea to black tea equals delicate tea to damaged tea.

Puerh Tea This particular tea is in a category of its own because of its unique and complex processing. Made from the larger leaves of the plant, they can be either sheng (raw, uncooked, green) or shu (cooked, black) and finished as loose leaf or compressed into a variety of shapes. If stored properly, Puerh teas are the only teas that improve with age and are often used as investment opportunities. Collectors have special caves, in which Puerh cakes mature for decades. Some people prefer to age Puerh cakes to save money to pay for their children's college, or because they consider it a safer investment option than the stock market. Puerh teas may be worth many thousands of dollars and the Puerh market is prone to counterfeiting, just like the Darjeeling or the Longjing markets.

Decaffeinated Tea Decaffeinated tea is very popular. This type of tea goes through a process to remove the caffeine. Since there are different levels of caffeine in different parts of the tea leaves, there are several different ways to decaffeinate tea. Just know that some tea lovers believe they can steep their tea, remove the water, steep again, and the tea will become decaffeinated—not true—this is an old wives' tale. In my opinion, tea can never truly be decaffeinated. Also, a word of caution—If the tea box lists "Mate" in its ingredients, the tea has caffeine. "Mate" is a South American caffeine plant.

Herbal Tea Herbal tea is not really tea at all. It is considered to be an infusion, or in Europe, tisane. Herbal infusions are made from combinations of herbs, leaves, flowers, plants, berries, and spices. They are naturally caffeine free and provide a wonderful alternative to caffeinated drinks and carbonated sodas. They are good both hot and cold. Rooibos or sometimes called Red Tea is naturally caffeine free and is a product from South Africa. It is sometimes spelled Rooibosch in accordance with the Dutch etymology but this does not change the pronunciation. Honeybush is a sister of Rooibos, with just a hint of honey flavor. In South Africa it is more common to drink Rooibos with cream (milk) and sugar, but elsewhere it is usually served without.

Traditionally used as "medicines," herbal teas may act as mild digestives, help lift depression, soothe you to sleep, and slenderize the physique. The myriad benefits of herbal teas also carry with them an element of caution. Exercise care in the amounts and kinds of herbal teas you drink. In the interest of safety, you should limit your intake to two or three cups per day, moderation being the key. Not all herbal teas are safe to drink as a beverage.

Beverage-Safe Herbs
  Alfalfa
  Catnip
  Chamomile
  Chicory root
  Elder flowers
  Fennel
  Fenugreek
  Ginger
  Goldenrod
  Hibiscus
  Lemongrass
  Linden flower
  Nettle
  Peppermint
  Rosehip
  Red and black raspberry
  Red clover
  Spearmint
  Slippery elm bark
  Yarrow

Roots
  Ginseng
  Turnip

Emma loves her catnip!

Store tea in special tins or light-proof glass or porcelain jars with tight covers. Place in cool, dark places away from heat and sunlight and away from odors.

Tea Pairings

Tea pairings with food are the perfect way to enhance the taste of a dish as well as the tea. The sensory experience explores the flavors and the aromas and creates the right balance between the food and the tea.

Fruits

Oolong Tea and Pineapples
The sweetness of the tea balances the acidity of the pineapple.

Oolong Tea and Strawberries
The fruitiness of each enhances the flavors.

Puerh Tea and Bananas
Bananas round out the roughness of Puerh.

Puerh Tea and Green Grapes
The freshness of the grapes added to the earthy Puerh produces a sweet effect.

Chocolates

Indian Chai Tea and Milk Chocolate
Both chocolate and chai are enhanced by the addition of sugar and cream. Pay attention to the way these two popular products complement each other as they coat the tongue.

Yunnan Black Tea and Dark Chocolate
It takes a dark chocolate to stand up to the rich earthy teas of Yunnan, China. Be sure to take a long breath of both before tasting. Your nose will give you an indication of what the tongue is about to experience.

Earl Grey Tea and Dark Truffle
The citrus notes of the world's favorite flavored tea blends perfectly with a delicious hand-rolled truffle. The rich, soft center of the truffle is made even more flavorful when paired with this historic English blend.

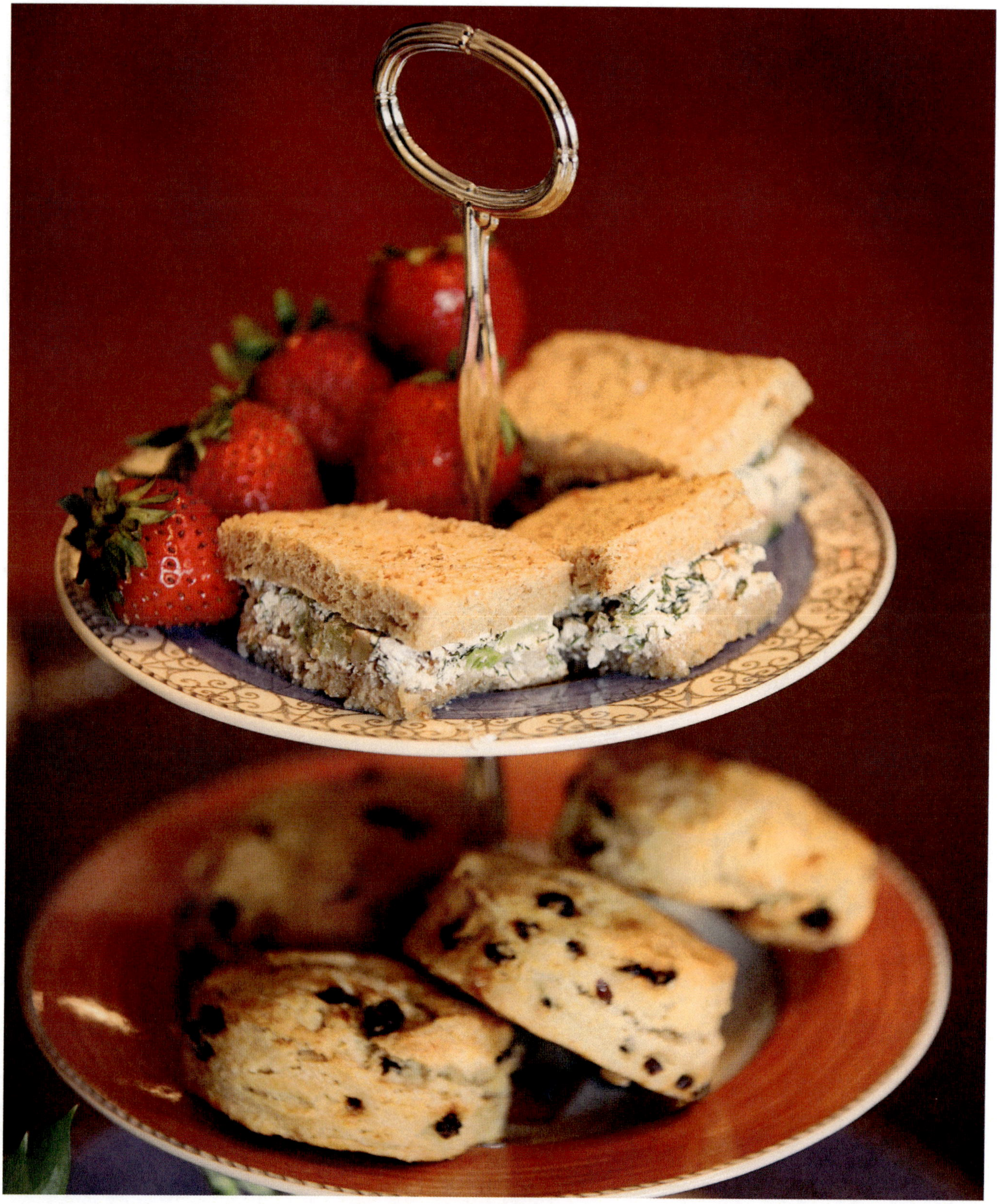

Savories/Sandwiches

Ham and Mustard The rich flavors of ham and mustard are perfectly complemented by a full-bodied tea such as a Second Flush Assam.

Cucumber A classic sandwich filling such as cucumber is well matched by the crisp, light and fresh flavors of the gently citrus White Darjeeling.

Chicken A well-loved favorite which is enhanced by Green Tea. This tea makes a perfect palate cleanser, and the vegetative flavor of green tea helps to boost the richness of the chicken.

Smoked Salmon and Cream Cheese The rich, strong flavors found in this classic sandwich filling are complemented by Smoky Lapsang Tea. The tea leaves found in this tea are dried over pinewood fires, creating a smoky taste that perfectly suits the flavor found in smoked salmon.

Teas

White Tea Lightly flavored foods—vegetable salads, cucumber salad, lightly flavored seafood, delicate sauces, peach-based desserts, Fior di latte cheese, and white chocolate

Green Tea Mild flavored foods—seafood (steamed or poached), chicken, rice, consomé, salads, fruits, melons, ice cream, flan, regular gouda cheese, and white chocolate

Oolong Tea More complex foods—grilled chicken, roasted meats, rich seafood, scallops, lobster, salmon, trout, desserts with maple syrup, fruit mousses, brie or camembert cheese, and fruit-based milk chocolate

Black Tea Full-flavored foods—spicy dishes, meat, game, eggs, potatoes, gravies, honey-based pastries, blue cheese, and milk chocolate

Puerh Tea Neutralizing tea—digestive benefits, preferred after large meals, heavy soups, rich cream meals, mushrooms, beets, no sweets, aged cheddar cheese, and dark chocolate

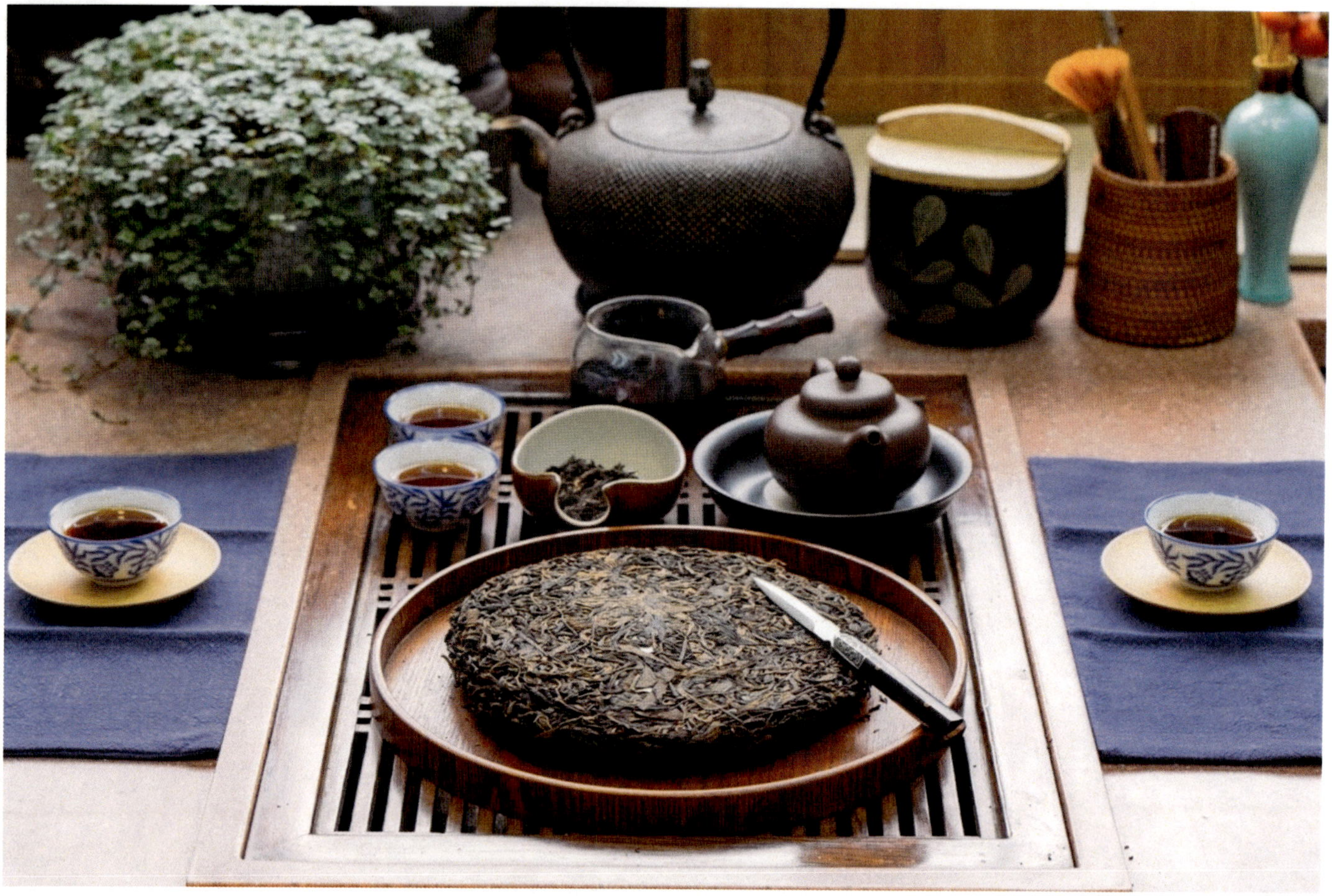

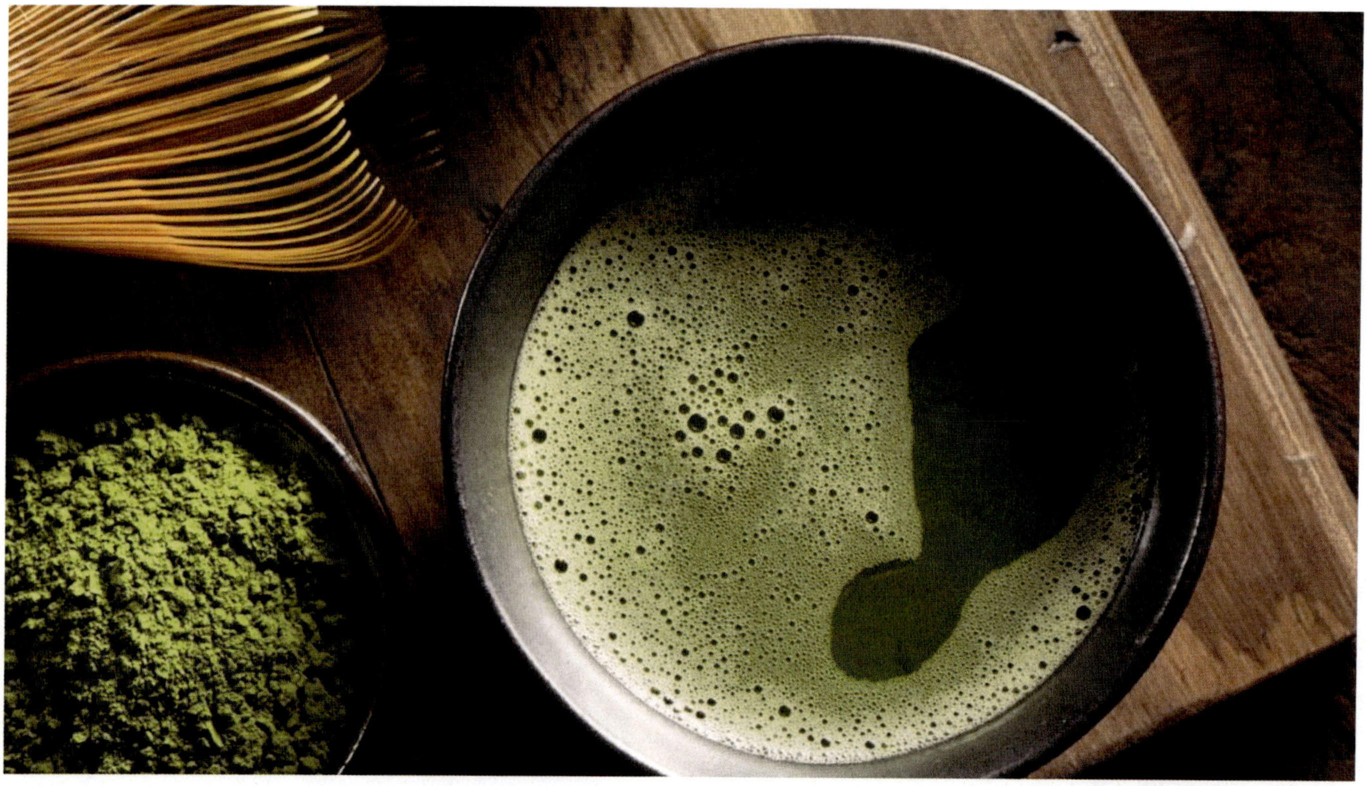

Tea Tastings

Only you, the tea taster, can say whether or not a tea is well made. Everyone has personal preferences and favorites, but here are general guidelines to follow when sampling a new tea:

Leaf Although this is usually performed by professional tea tasters, understanding the size and shape of the leaf, as well as the location of the leaf on the stalk affects the quality. Tea graders also evaluate the twist or roll of the tea leaves. Wiry and well-twisted leaves are favorable.

Liquor Liquor refers to the brightness of color and clarity of the infusion. Fine black teas are referred to as having a coppery or bright appearance.

Aroma Aroma refers to whether or not the tea has a pleasant smell. Fresh teas have a lively, natural fragrance which is lacking in older teas. A tea with great aroma is prized by many tea drinkers, yet it may not have the body that some people expect in their tea.

Astringency Astringency refers to a sharpness, bitterness, or edge to the tea's taste. Some highly prized teas, such as Darjeelings, are known to have a higher degree of astringency, giving the tea a brisk, lively, desirable taste. The most effective ways to control astringency are to use high-quality water, effective heating methods, and proper amounts of time for brewing.

Body Body refers to whether or not a tea feels thick in the mouth, such as an Assam tea. It may also be very light or watery similar to many green teas.

Taste Tea tasters seek complex flavor characteristics, and they evaluate the tea's body or strength. Clean and brisk are desirable; flat, dull, and sweaty are less desirable. The most critical flavor with tea is the lack of harshness. Younger, fresher tea leaves have a mellow infusion. Some teas, such as Lapsang, Souchong or Russian Caravan, have a smoky flavor and taste. Other flavored teas that you may recognize are jasmine teas or Earl Grey tea, which is flavored with oil of bergamot. Your preference for drinking teas plain, or for adding cream, lemon, and/or sugar, will affect the taste of the tea. Also, the foods that you consume with your tea can greatly affect how your tea tastes.

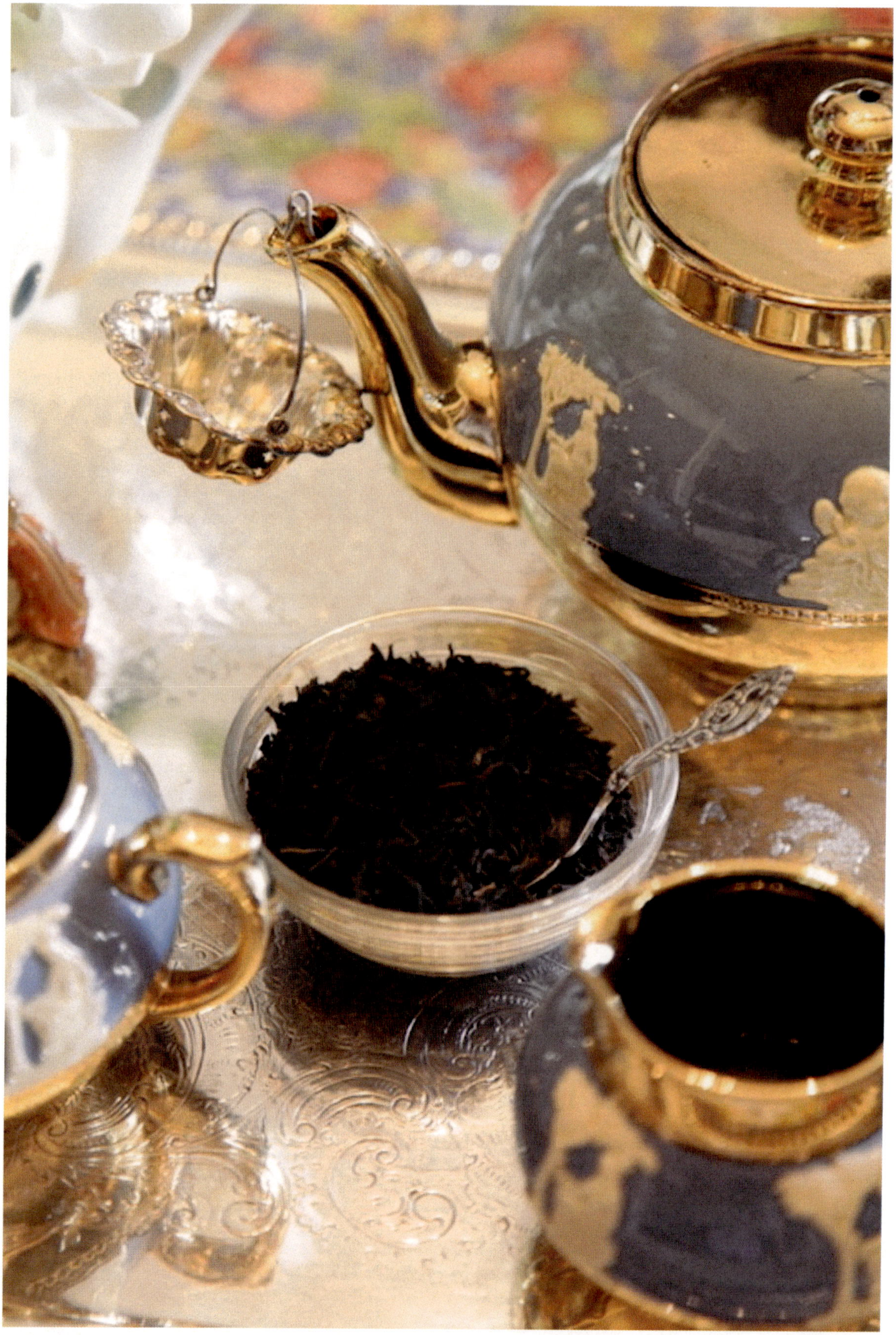

Preparing a "Proper" Tea at Home

epending on the formality of your tea, invitations may be sent out three to six weeks ahead for formal teas and two weeks ahead for informal teas. Invitations should be engraved and include the host or hostess' name, date, time, place, and guest of honor. They should be written in third person—Ms. Smith requests the pleasure of your company. See chapter on Easy Entertaining for more detailed information.

Reminder cards may be sent out approximately ten days before the scheduled tea.

If hosting an impromptu tea, inviting may be done on the telephone, particularly when it is less than two weeks away.

Tea Style Buffet When preparing a tea style buffet, the buffet should be covered with a traditional white linen or lace tea cloth. Decorate with fresh flowers. Pretty china certainly adds to the festive feeling and does not have to match. Also include embroidered serviettes. If using a silver tea service, ensure it is well polished.

Include a large silver tea tray without a tea cloth. On the tray, place a teapot filled with freshly brewed tea kept warm by either an alcohol lamp or a tea cozy. Include a pitcher of very hot water for those who would like to dilute their tea or to add more hot water to the teapot, a tea strainer if you use loose tea, a waste bowl for spent tea leaves and cold tea, a cream pitcher with cream (milk), a sugar bowl with lump sugar and sugar tongs, and if space permits, a plate of lemon slices with a lemon fork.

On the buffet, place the china, flatware, serviettes, savories, scones with assorted fruit spreads, lemon curd, clotted cream, and beautifully displayed petits fours.

As host or hostess assign one or two of your friends who are familiar with the protocol of serving tea to stand in for you at the buffet and pour tea for your guests. The pourer ("Mother") should ask each guest what he or she wants in his or her tea, such as cream, sugar, etc., and then put in the ingredients. Guests may return to the buffet for more tea after everyone has been served.

Also include a table for used dishes.

Tea Style Buffet Setting

For a more intimate tea, you should place all necessary tea equipage on a large silver tray (no cloth on tray) such as: tea plates, serviettes, flatware, teacups with saucers, and teaspoons. Include on the tray a teapot filled with freshly brewed tea kept warm by either an alcohol lamp or a tea cozy, a pitcher of very hot water for those who would like to dilute their tea or to add more hot water to the teapot, a tea strainer if you use loose tea, a waste bowl for spent tea leaves and cold tea, a cream pitcher with cream (milk), a sugar bowl with lump sugar and sugar tongs, and a plate of lemon slices with a lemon fork. As the host or hostess, you should pour tea for the guests.

Intimate Tea Tray Setting

You may enjoy this tea in a more private area such as the living room or out in the patio.

When friends are invited in advance to your home for tea, tea bags should not be used, and they certainly should not be used for a large tea either. Use tea bags only if you meet someone during the day and invite them home with you to enjoy a cup of tea.

The British tea tradition makes the hostess "Mother" or allows the hostess to name a guest Mother. This has evolved from Mothers serving tea to their families. To be asked to serve as Mother is a compliment to a guest. Mother asks each guest how he or she takes their tea and serves it to them as requested. Think of the Mother as the pourer. Some people do not like their tea strong. For these people, one needs to keep a pot of hot water and if asked for their tea to be weak, the Mother dilutes it with a little of the water.

Making a Perfect Pot of Tea

The round shape of the teapot was designed by the Chinese who used a musk melon as a model. The shape is different from a coffee or chocolate pot. The lower portion or body of the teapot is rounded to ensure the tea leaves have the proper room for expansion during the infusion process. The lower placement of the spout on the vessel allows for the tea to be poured without interfering with the leaves.

To make a perfect pot of tea, boil fresh cold water in a kettle. Cold water is essential because it has more oxygen content and gives the tea a fuller flavor. While the water is boiling, warm the teapot with hot water. Once the teapot is warmed, pour out the water and put in the tea leaves. Use one teaspoon of tea leaves or one tea bag per cup of tea. Once the water is boiling, carry the teapot over to the kettle and pour the water into the teapot immediately—boiling water drops in temperature the moment it is removed from the flame. Cover the teapot with a tea cozy to keep it hot. Let the tea brew three to five minutes depending upon the type of tea. Agitate occasionally.

Since measuring spoons do not always work because some tea leaves are bigger than others, a better way to measure would be with a gram scale. Measure two grams of tea per cup.

When measuring how many cups there are in a teapot, measure five ounces per cup instead of eight ounces.

Always brew by the clock, not by the color. Different teas and herbal infusions require different steeping or infusion times. White, green, and oolong teas steep for about one to two minutes while black and chai teas and herbal infusions steep for about three to seven minutes. Steeping time also depends on several factors such as the tea family, the leaf size, and the amount of twist or roll in the leaf. Most tea merchants include brewing instructions on their labels. Every tea will taste better if it is "brewed rather than stewed."

Tips on Serving Tea

* Serve the tea in the following ways: plain, with cream (usually when the word "cream" is used, it really means milk), with sugar, with cream and sugar, with lemon, with lemon and sugar, with honey, or with honey and cream.

* Never serve cream and lemon together in tea. The citric acid of the lemon will cause the cream to curdle.

* If a guest requests lemon, pour the guest a cup of tea and place the lemon slice in the cup. If the guest desires another cup of tea, remove the used slice of lemon. As hostess, pour another cup of tea for the guest and place another lemon slice in the cup.

* Used lemon slices are placed on a separate saucer, not on the teacup saucer. Never use a teaspoon to press the lemon slice after it is placed in a cup. Untouched, the oil from the peel and the fruit will provide the desired essence.

* Sugar is served in the form of cubes for neatness.

* If a guest requests sugar and lemon, add the sugar first. Otherwise the citric acid of the lemon will prevent the sugar from dissolving.

Milk in first or milk in last—the continuing debate—you decide: The butler in the popular 1970s television program Upstairs, Downstairs kindly gave the following advice to the household servants who were arguing about the virtues of milk before or after the tea is poured: "Those of us downstairs put the milk in first, while those upstairs put the milk in last."

According to the English writer Evelyn Waugh, "All nannies and many governesses put the milk in first." And, by the way, Queen Elizabeth II adds the milk last.

The Pinky Dilemma—The age-old question: to crook your little finger or tuck it in. When tea arrived in Europe in the sixteen hundreds, it was served in small (think demitasse) cups without handles. The cup drew very hot, and the tea drinker was not disposed to burn ALL of one's fingers. When the handle was added to the cup, fingers still remained poised away from the cup and the custom came down over the centuries, no longer with a purpose except to be what the rich and pretentious considered "proper."

Clean your teapot by pouring out tea and immediately rinse with clean water. Turn upside down to drain. Dry the outside and the inside. To remove tea stains, use a solution of baking soda and hot water and soak overnight. You may also use a very small amount of bleach. Let it sit for a couple of minutes. Rinse with water and wash with soap and rinse again. Again, dry the outside and the inside.

Tea Table Setting

Iced Tea
12 teaspoons of tea leaves or 12 tea bags - 2 quarts cold, fresh tap water

The rule of thumb when making iced tea is to use 50 percent more tea than when making hot tea. Pour 1 quart of water into a saucepan and 1 quart of water into a 2-quart pitcher. Heat the water in the pan until boiling. Remove the pan from the heat, add the tea bags to the pan, and let sit for 10 minutes. Remove the bags from the pan and pour the tea concentrate into the pitcher of cold water. Cover and refrigerate until cold (approximately for two to three hours). Because of tea solids, tea made this way sometimes becomes cloudy. The flavor isn't affected, but if this bothers you, pour a small amount of boiling water into the tea. This should clear it up.

Sun-Brewed Tea
1 quart cold, fresh tap water - 6 teaspoons of tea leaves or 6 tea bags

Place the cold water in a glass container. Put the tea bags into the water, cover, and set out in the sun for two hours. Serve over ice or refrigerate until ready to use.

Proper Way to Serve and Drink Iced Tea Iced tea is served in a tall glass with ice cubes and placed on a saucer with a long iced teaspoon. The iced teaspoon is placed at 5 o'clock on the saucer with the spoon bowl facing up. If you use the iced teaspoon to stir your tea after adding sugar, place it back on the saucer. Never place it on a table top; it will stain fine linens. If you are not provided a saucer and you have used your spoon, rest the spoon in the iced-tea glass. When you want to take a sip, grasp the spoon between the second and third fingers of your hand while holding the stemware and sip the tea. Finish position is 5 o'clock on the saucer with the spoon bowl facing up.

Specialty Teas Most specialty teas have black tea for a base and are flavored with spices, fruits, or other ingredients such as almonds, cinnamon, lemon, or mint. These teas are distinguished from herbal infusions by the fact that they contain caffeine. They are also made with distilled essences of oils and are available in a large variety of flavors.

Below are two possible alternatives to making fruit teas:

Put a spoonful of fruit preserves in your cup before adding the tea. Keep in mind that doing so will sweeten the tea.

Put a slice of lemon or orange rind (a two-by-one quarter-inch slice per cup) in the teapot with the tea leaves. Pour in boiling water and let the mixture steep for five minutes. The boiling water will release the fruit oil, thereby lightly flavoring the tea.

Tea Mote Spoons were used prior to the Tea Caddy Spoons and the initial use was most likely to lift the tea leaves from the caddy and gently shake or tap the spoon allowing the dust or mote to drop prior to use in the pot. Tea in the seventeenth century and most of the eighteenth century was supplied in a rather crude form with large leaves and a great deal of dust. As tea became less crude, the spoons began to be used to remove any foreign leaves from the brewed tea. The sharp pointed end would have been used to dislodge blockages from the inside of the spout of the teapot.

Stirring a cup of tea is done gently by moving the teaspoon in a small arc back and forth in the center of the cup. Do not allow the teaspoon to touch the sides or rim of the cup.

Sugar in the eighteenth century (Jane Austen's time) was kept locked up because it was very expensive. It was sold in many grades, from the highly refined pure white sugar, which only the well-off could afford, down to the darkest of brown sugars used by the poor. Granulated sugar only recently had been invented and was not yet widely available. Sugar was molded into large, cone-shaped loaves weighing several pounds each that had to be broken up or grated before it could be used. Sugar cubes would not be invented until 1843. If people wanted sugar for tea, they had to first break it into irregular lumps with special tools called "sugar nippers," from which practices comes the traditional question—

"One lump or two?"

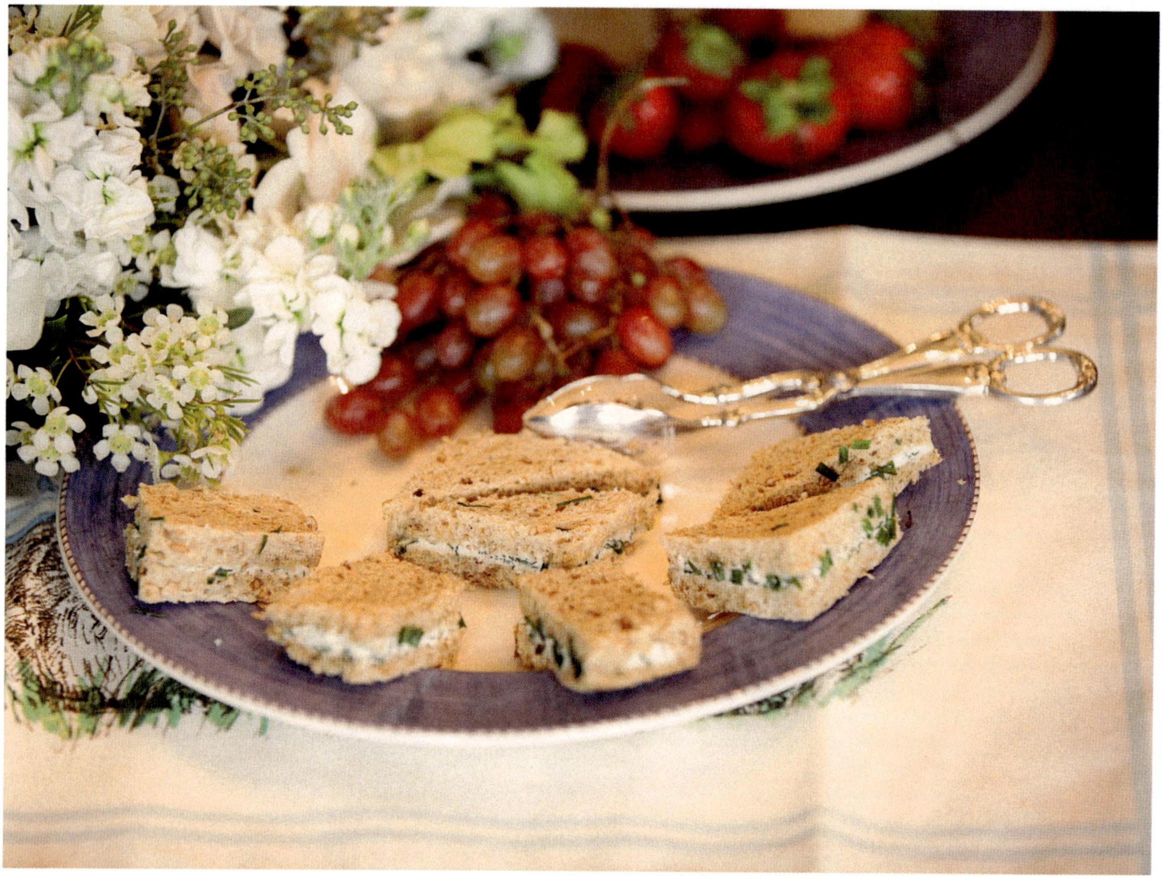

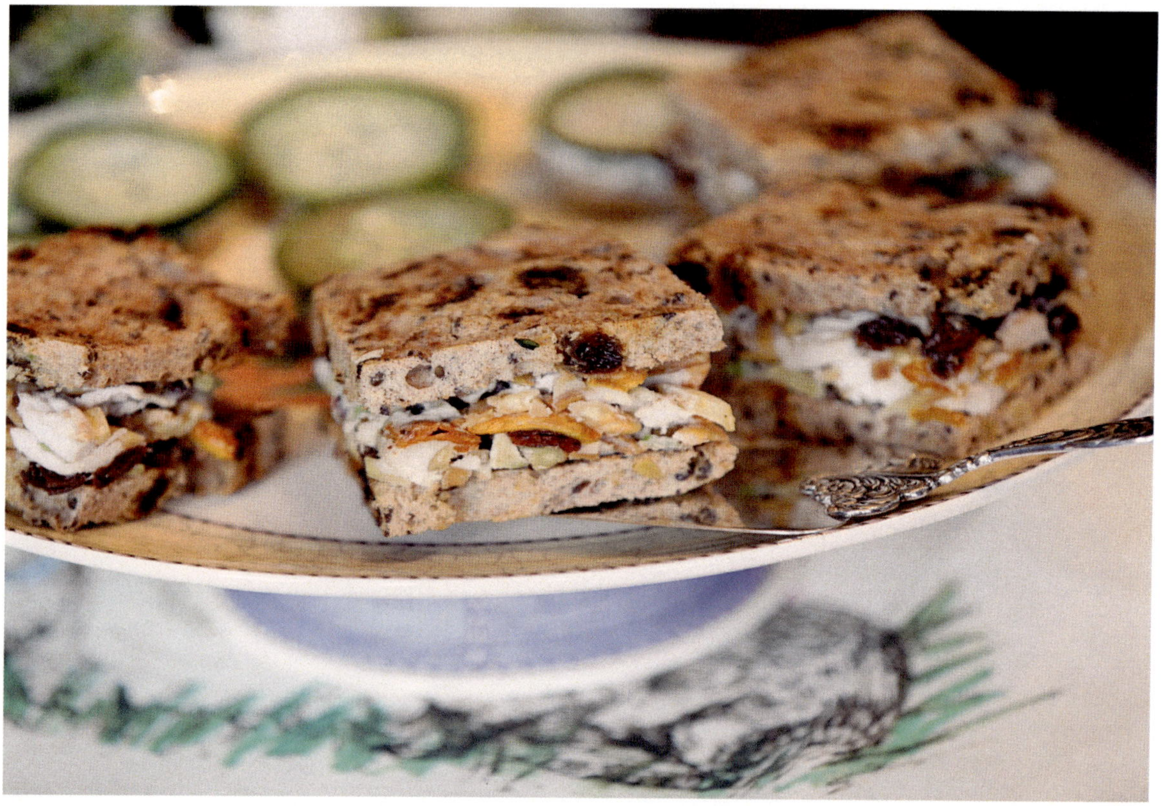

Dining with Savories

Guidelines to Prepare, Serve, and Dine

The notorious eighteenth-century gambler John Montagu, Fourth Earl of Sandwich, is credited with inventing the sandwich. In 1762, when Montagu was forty-four years old, his passion for gambling kept him at the gaming tables for twenty-four hours straight. To keep gambling, he ordered sliced meats and cheeses served to him between pieces of bread. This method enabled him to eat with one hand and gamble with the other. Tea sandwiches, or savories, are tasty tidbits eaten first to blunt your appetite. They may be open-faced or closed sandwiches consisting of cucumbers, chicken salad, salmon, hummus, tomatoes, and so forth.

To prepare savories, begin with fresh, thinly sliced bread. Savories may be either open-faced or closed. Every slice of bread (white or wheat) should be covered with a very thin coating of butter. This stops the filling from leaking through, thus preventing the bread from becoming soggy. Use real butter, not margarine. Spread the filling on the bread. Trim the crusts off and cut the savory in fours, threes, or other interesting shapes. As mentioned in previous sections, fillings might include minced chicken or ham salad, cream cheese and watercress, and smoked salmon. Always serve cucumber savories; they are refreshing and cut through the richness of other foods. Make eight savories per person.

To prepare the savories earlier in the day or the day before, arrange them on doily-lined plates or trays and cover them with waxed paper and dampened tea towels until ready to serve. Serve on beautiful serving plates with serving utensils.

Savories are eaten as you would eat "finger foods." Finger foods are categorized as foods to be eaten with one's left-hand fingers. You may either break off a piece of the savory and convey it to your mouth with your left hand or pick up the savory with your left hand and bite a small piece of it. Your left hand is used for finger foods in order to keep the right hand clean to hold the teacup or to serve tea.

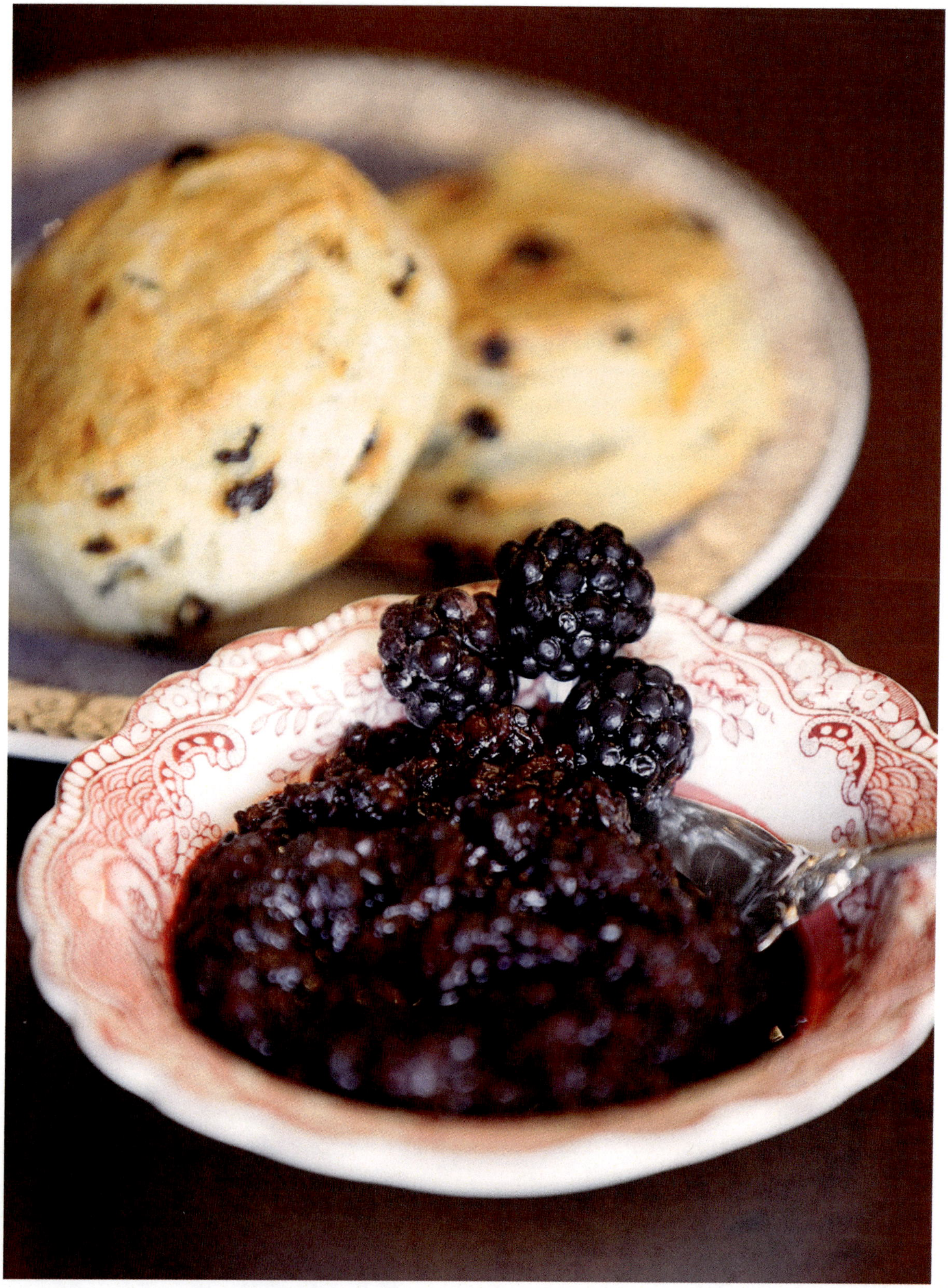

Dining with Scones

Guidelines to Serve and Dine

cones originated in Scotland. The original Gaelic word sgonn (which sounds like gone) means a shapeless lump of dough. The first scones were baked free form on a "girdle," or griddle, over a fire. They were originally made from oat or barley flour because wheat has never grown well in the Scottish Highlands. In time, scone dough would be formed into a circle and cut into farls (fourths), much the way we shape them today.

Serve scones in a decorative cloth-lined basket to keep them warm or serve them individually to each guest. Along with the scones, serve jams, fruit spreads or homemade preserves, fruit butters, lemon curd, and clotted cream. If a clotted cream substitute is needed, use freshly whipped cream.

Jams, fruit spreads, preserves, lemon curd, and clotted cream are sometimes served from a bowl. You may place the serving spoon in the bowl for rest position and finish position. If served from stemware, rest position and finish position dictate that you never leave the serving spoon in the stemware. Place the serving spoon to the right of the stemware preferably on a plate or saucer underneath it.

The proper way to eat a scone is with one's fingers. Split the scone in half across the girth with your fingers. Place a spoonful of fruit spread or lemon curd and clotted cream onto the small tea plate with serving utensils. Spread a little fruit spread or lemon curd on a bite-size portion of the scone's crumb face with your dessert knife. Add clotted cream and eat just that portion.

A second method is to break off a bite-size piece with your fingers just in case you are unable to split the scone in half. Spread a little fruit spread or lemon curd and clotted cream on the piece broken off and convey it to your mouth with your fingers.

The last method is quite easy. This method is used when scones have been drizzled with fruit syrup. In this method, you may eat the scone in either Continental or American style. For either Continental or American style, the first step is to secure the scone with a dessert fork and use a dessert knife to cut one bite-size piece at a time.

Clotted cream and Devonshire cream originated in Cornwall and Devonshire, England around the thirteen hundreds. In these areas, cows graze on fertile lands and are fed and bred to produce rich, creamy milk. Devonshire cream is 48% milk fat and clotted cream is 55% milk fat. Jam was introduced by England.

Devon! Cornwall! What do you put first on a scone—clotted cream or jam? In Devonshire, clotted cream is spread first and jam second. In Cornwall, jam is spread first and clotted cream second.

Dining with Petits Fours

Guidelines to Serve and Dine

erve petits fours on decorative plates with serving utensils. Again, you may eat the petits fours as you would eat finger foods unless the petits fours are overfilled with cream or otherwise unwieldy.

For unwieldy petits fours, you may eat them in either Continental or American style. For Continental and American style, the first step is to secure the petit four with a dessert fork and use a dessert knife to cut one bite-size piece at a time.

You may also eat them with a dessert fork and a dessert spoon. For this method of dining, follow Continental style. The dessert fork is held in your left hand with tines facing down and the dessert spoon is held in your right hand. You may eat the petit four with either your dessert fork or your dessert spoon.

Tea and Croquet

Anna, Duchess of Bedford, became well known for her at-home tea parties in about 1860; and what else would one do at a tea party, play croquet!

Croquet was initially a game for the well-to-do Europeans. The object of croquet is to complete the course of nine wickets and hit the finishing stake before your opponents do. A ball scores a wicket by passing through each wicket, however, there are rules governing the manner and means by which a player may enter a wicket.

When croquet first came to the United States, tea and croquet parties were an important part of daily social graces. During the summer at country estates, tea was held outside. What beautiful occasions these must have been.

Although we no longer have to contend with étiquette concerning ladies moving across the court with their long skirts, there are still rules of polite and correct behavior that should be maintained during a croquet match.

Picnic Tea

Pack a Tea Basket for a Lovely Outdoor Event

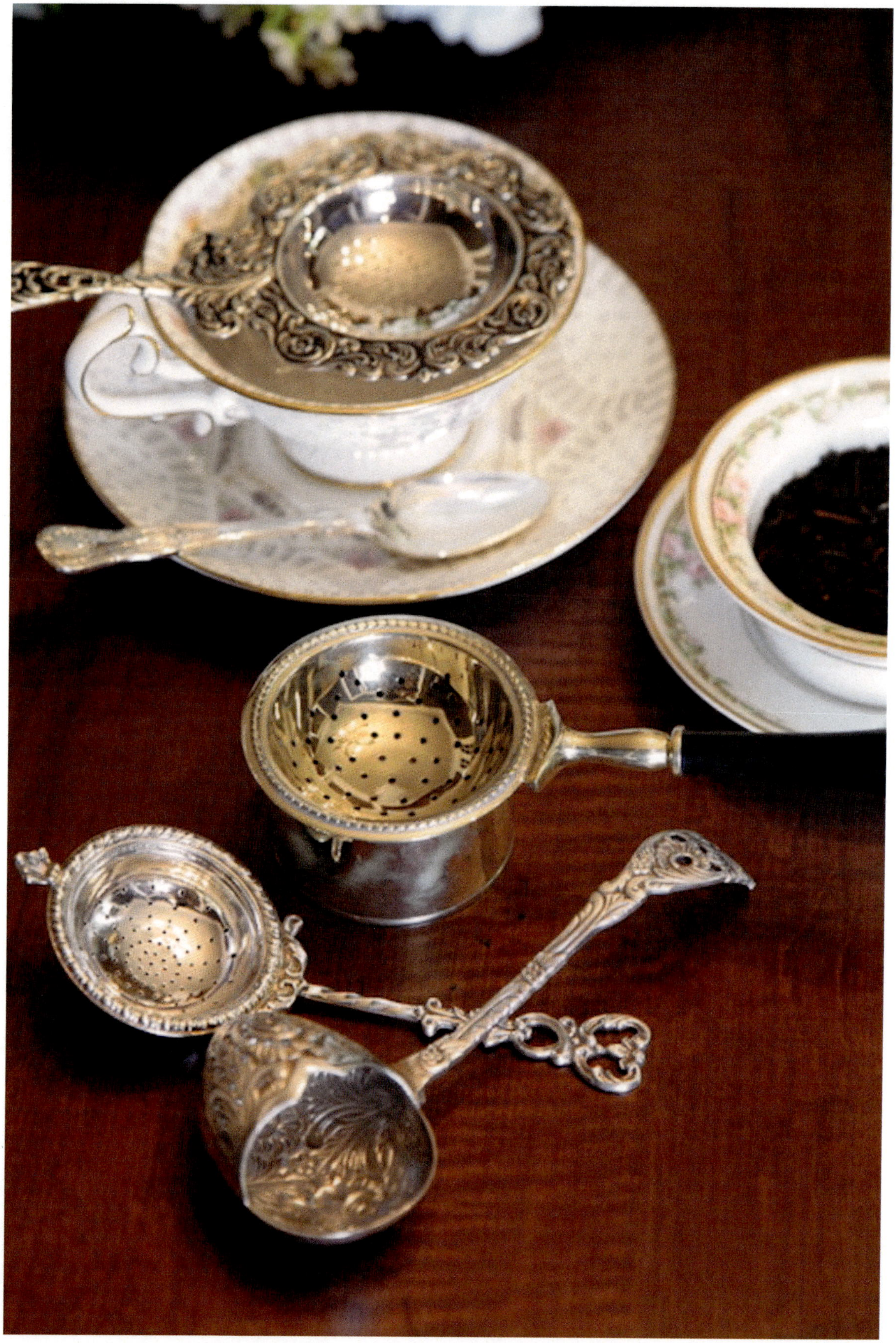

Enjoying Tea from a Teapot in a Teahouse or Restaurant

When served a tea bag with a small teapot of water and a cup and saucer, remove the tea bag from the paper wrapper and place the tea bag in the teapot. Request a separate saucer to hold the paper wrapper. Allow the tea to steep until it reaches the strength you prefer. After three to five minutes, pour a small amount into the cup to test the strength. Do not pick up the tea bag by the tab on the string and jiggle it up and down to hasten the process. This looks tacky and gives the appearance of impatience. Do not remove the tea bag from the teapot.

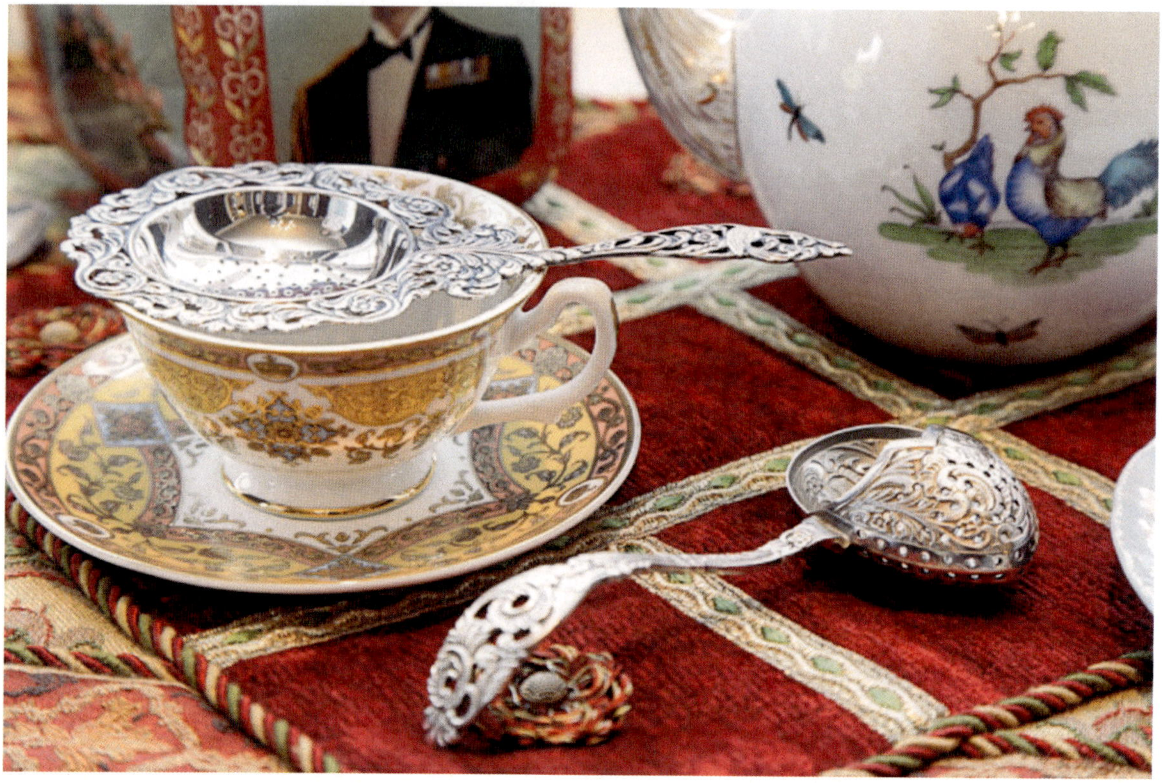

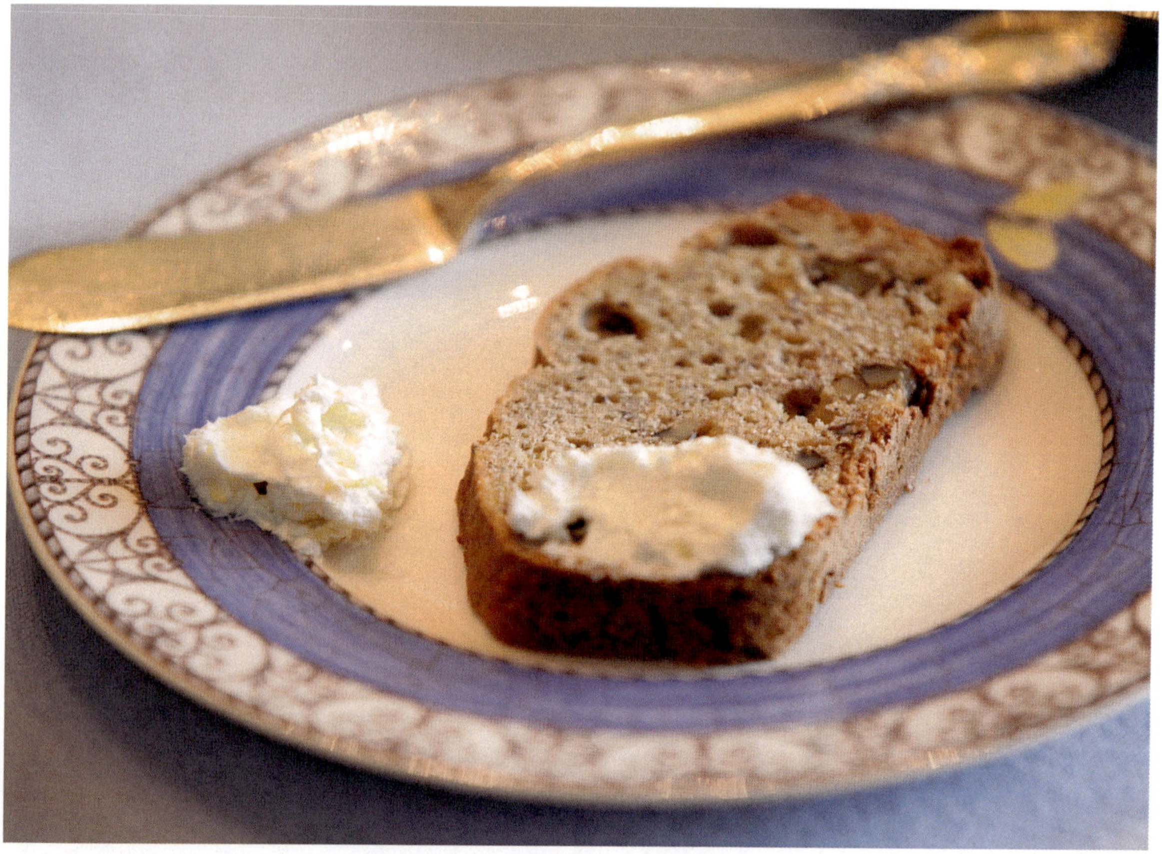

Enjoying Tea from a Teacup in a Teahouse or Restaurant

When served a cup of hot water with a tea bag placed on a saucer, remove the tea bag from its paper wrapper and place the tea bag in the cup of hot water. Request a separate saucer to hold the paper wrapper and used tea bag. Allow the tea to steep until it reaches the strength you prefer. Remove the used tea bag from the cup. Place the used tea bag on the separate saucer you requested. Never attempt to drain a tea bag by winding the string around a spoon.

Stirring one's teaspoon in a cup should be done quietly moving back and forth in the center of the cup.

Polite Society School of Étiquette

The Art of

Timeless Étiquette,

Graceful Dining Manners,

&

Afternoon Tea

As founder and director of the *Polite Society School of Étiquette*, it is my hope that *The Art of Timeless Étiquette, Graceful Dining Manners, & Afternoon Tea* will guide you in the intricate dance of manners, customs, and basic social graces in the world of étiquette and will give you the self-confidence of learning gracious and proper manners.

With warm wishes and thanks,
Bernadette Michelle Petrotta

Made in the USA
Middletown, DE
10 November 2021